TIME AND MEDIA MARKETS

TIME AND MEDIA MARKETS

Edited by

Alan B. Albarran
University of North Texas

Angel Arrese
University of Navarra

LEA LAWRENCE ERLBAUM ASSOCIATES, PUBLISHERS
2003   Mahwah, New Jersey   London

Copyright © 2003 by Lawrence Erlbaum Associates, Inc.

Cover design by Kathryn Houghtaling Lacey

Lawrence Erlbaum Associates, Inc., Publishers
10 Industrial Avenue
Mahwah, NJ 07430

Library of Congress Cataloging-in-Publication Data

Time and Media Markets / edited by Alan B. Albarran, Angel Arrese.
                           p. cm.—(LEA's Communication Series)
  Includes bibliographical references and index.
ISBN 0-8058-4113-X (cloth : alk. paper)
1. Mass Media—Marketing. 2. Time Management. I. Albarran, Alan B.
  II. Arrese, Angel.   III. Series

P96.M36 T56 2002
302.23'068'8—dc21   2001000000
                                              CIP

Books published by Lawrence Erlbaum Associates are printed on acid-
free paper, and their bindings are chosen for strength and durability.

Printed in the United States of America
10 9 8 7 6 5 4 3 2 1

*To Don Alfonso Nieto
and my good friends at the
University of Navarra*
—*Alan B. Albarran*

To my wife, Christina
—*Angel Arrese*

CONTENTS

PREFACE

The concept of time has captured the imagination of philosophers and scientists through the ages. Time is something we all experience, and often take for granted. We encounter different experiences with time as we advance through the life cycle. When children grow up, they are almost oblivious to time. If anything, they can't wait to "grow up" some day, so they can be like adults.

Yet, when we become adults, many people complain that their lives are too busy and there are too many demands on their time. We struggle to manage our time, and seek a balance among the pressures of work, family, and rest. As people move into retirement, time becomes more precious as we begin to recognize our own mortality.

People born since the middle of the 20th century have lived their lives in an increasingly media-saturated environment that competes for their time. As new forms of media technology have diffused, people tend to spend even more time with the media, in the form of television and motion pictures, sound recordings, books, newspapers, magazines, and the Internet. For many adults, media-related activities comprise over one third of their time.

The media industries are driven by time. Programs must be produced to air at certain times, whereas printed works are also subject to time and distribution deadlines. Many industries are supported by their ability to sell time (and space) to advertisers, so that the advertisers can gain access to audiences that consume media content. As chapter 1 of this edited volume illustrates, time and media are linked together, and are worthy of our attention and study.

This collection of chapters on different aspects of time and media markets was developed from the third World Media Economics Conference held at the University of Navarra in Pamplona, Spain, in May 2000. The title of that conference was "Time and Media Markets," and scholars were invited to present works for consideration in the conference program related to the theme, as well as open papers.

We were fortunate to serve as coordinators of the conference, along with other faculty from the University of Navarra's Department of Media Management. The conference was very successful, and the papers presented that were related to the conference theme illustrated a diverse range of interests and methodologies. We felt it was important to try and share these works. Thus, after the conference was finished, the coordinators reviewed the papers from the conference that best illustrated the conference theme, and prepared a proposal to turn the papers into an edited volume of research.

Because the conference was co-sponsored by the *Journal of Media Economics,* we wanted to give the journal's publisher, Lawrence Erlbaum Associates, the opportunity to review the proposal. That process provided a number of helpful suggestions by the reviewers, who also felt a work addressing the topic of time and media markets was needed and could make a contribution to the literature.

In short, LEA contracted to publish the book that you now hold. However, this is not simply a collection of papers or proceedings from a conference; only nine papers were selected for inclusion in this edited volume, every chapter went through at least one revision, and some chapters were extensively revised based on both the reviewers' comments and the direction given by the co-editors. In addition, an introductory chapter and a summary chapter were prepared just for this text.

PLAN OF THE BOOK

The introductory chapter, written by the co-editors, presents a philosophical look at the concept of time and its application to media markets. The chapter also reviews the literature from several key journals in the field, to understand how time has been examined in the study of media markets.

Chapter 2, written by Jacques Durand, is a philosophical examination of media and the representation of time. In chapter 3, Daniel G. McDonald and John W. Dimmick utilize the biological theory of the niche as a framework to examine competition between the Internet and television.

Chapter 4, authored by Robert G. Picard and Mikko Grönlund, examines temporal aspects of media distribution for the media industries, and how time affects their activities.

In chapter 5, Dan Shaver and Mary Alice Shaver look at the impact of increasing media industry consolidation and convergence on managerial effectiveness. The authors examine the activities of eight companies over a 10-year time period.

Chapter 6, authored by Mercedes Medina, looks at how CNN and its cache of various news channels approaches time, especially from a managerial context.

In Chapter 7, David H. Goff looks at Internet access in the United Kingdom and European continent to examine the cost of time for online access.

The field of advertising and, specifically, media planning is the focus of chapter 8, written by Francisco Javier Pérez-Latre. The author also considers the impact of the Internet on the advertising process of buying time and space in the media.

Chapter 9, authored by Alfonso Nieto, uses the country of Spain for an analysis of media markets as time markets.

In chapter 10, Patricia F. Phalen analyzes the exchange of time and money in the television market for advertising, reviewing the various strategies and consequences in the information market.

Finally, in chapter 11, the co-editors provide a summary of the research presented in this volume, and offer some directions for future research on the topic of time and media markets.

ACKNOWLEDGMENTS

Many people contributed to the development of the 2000 World Media Economics Conference that was the genesis for this book. At the University of Navarra, we are particularly grateful to Don Alfonso Nieto, Dean Alfonso Sanchez Tabernero, Mercedes Medina, and the rest of professors of the Media Management Department.

Our individual contributors were a pleasure to work with, and they were very responsive in meeting deadlines and answering queries and concerns from the editors.

We thank the anonymous reviewers who provided helpful comments on the initial proposal, as well as Series Editor Jennings Bryant, of the University of Alabama, for his insight and guidance. Also, we greatly appreciate the support of Editor Linda Bathgate at LEA, who was helpful and encouraging throughout the preparation of the book.

Finally, we are fortunate to be blessed with loving families who are supportive of the time we spend on research and writing. Thanks to Beverly, Beth, and Amanda, and to Christina, Angel, Isabel, and Pablo.

Our hope is that this work will inspire others to think about time and media markets in new ways, and encourage further research into this important topic. Likewise, we hope that readers will gain some new perspectives on their own time, and how they use this scarce and precious resource we all share.

—*Alan B. Albarran*
—*Angel Arrese*
November, 2001

1

TIME AND MEDIA MARKETS:
AN INTRODUCTION[1]

Alan B. Albarran
University of North Texas

Angel Arrese
University of Navarra

This introductory chapter provides an overview of the concept of time and its application to the study of media markets and industries. Our goal in this chapter is to provide a context that will enable the reader to understand the theoretical and practical approaches that can be used to study the temporal dimension. Other chapters in this text examine different aspects of time as applied to specific media markets and media-related situations.

Why should we be interested in the concept of time and its application to media markets? Time is a limited resource. There are only 24 hours in a day, 7 days in a week, and 52 weeks in a year. Our lives revolve around time—time for work, time for friends and family, time for rest and sleep, and time for other activities. People complain that there is not enough time to do everything that needs to be done. Humans experience stress and health problems due to their inability to manage time.

Despite our time-driven lives, we spend a considerable amount of time engaged in media-related activities (see Table 1.1). This is especially true for

---

[1]For questions, contact the first author: Dr. Alan B. Albarran, Department of Radio, Television and Film, University of North Texas, P. O. Box 310589, Denton, TX 76203. Phone: 940-565-2537. E-mail: albarran@unt.edu

TABLE 1.1
Annual Media Usage Among U.S. Adults (18 and older)
for Selected Categories

Hours per Person per Year	*1995*	*1997*	*1999 (est.)*	*2001 (est.)*	*2003 (est.)*
Total hours	3,391	3,371	3,448	3,523	3,587
Television*	1,575	1,561	1,579	1,595	1,610
Radio	1,091	1,082	1,037	1,014	992
Recorded music	289	265	288	300	319
Daily newspapers	165	159	154	151	149
Consumer books	99	95	94	97	99
Consumer magazines	84	82	81	79	78
Home video**	45	50	57	62	66
Movies in theaters	12	13	13	14	15
Home video games	24	36	48	65	67
Consumer Internet access	7	28	97	146	192

Source: Adapted from *Statistical Abstract of the United States* (2000).
*Television includes all forms of television (broadcast stations, networks, cable, satellite, and premium or pay-per-view services).
**Home video is limited to playback of prerecorded tapes/discs.
Note: Given that a year contains 8,736 hours, U.S. media usage has grown from a total of 38% of total time in 1995 to an estimated 41% of time by 2003.

citizens of the United States and other developed nations of the world, for whom there are many options for media-related entertainment and information. Individuals can watch multiple channels of television delivered by terrestrial, cable, or satellite. There are daily and weekly newspapers, hundreds of magazine titles, and fiction and nonfiction books to read. We watch movies and listen to recorded music. The Internet combines text, graphics, audio, and video to create a rich environment that also requires our time and attention.

Using the time estimated for media consumption, we can offer some assumptions concerning adults who are employed full time about the percentage of their time spent in media use compared with other primary activities such as work, sleep and rest, and other activities. These data are presented in Table 1.2.

These numbers were derived as follows. If a person works 8 hours a day for 44 weeks (allowing time off for holidays and vacation schedules), he or she would labor an estimated 1,760 hours. If a person sleeps an average 7

TABLE 1.2
Assumptions on Estimated Time Allocation Among Adults for 2003

Category	Estimated Annual Hours	Percentage
Media usage	3,523	41%
Work	1,760	20%
Rest/sleep	2,555	29%
Other time	905	10%

hours a day, he or she would amass a total of 2,555 hours of rest per year. The remaining hours (905) represent time for other activities. Obviously, media usage can occur in conjunction with either work or other time. In any event, as these tables illustrate, time and media are inexorably linked to one another—and are deserving of our attention and scholarly examination.

This chapter is organized along four main sections. First, we begin with a general discussion of time, and how our understanding of time has evolved from both philosophical and historical perspectives. After this orientation, we review the literature regarding the concept of time and the study of media markets. Next, we examine how the concept of time has been researched in a number of media journals. Finally, we discuss the implications of this examination and offer conclusions regarding the research on time and media markets.

UNDERSTANDING TIME

Time is central to every human being. We are uniquely aware of time in our personal lives. We experience the passage of time as we evolve through the life cycle. Time is in many ways a puzzling mystery. We know there is a past because we have experienced a past. We know the present, because it is in the present that we live. We anticipate the future, whether it is the next day or the next week, month, or year. Finally, we know that someday our time on earth will come to an end with death.

The concept of time, and defining it, have confounded philosophers and scholars for the ages. It is impractical in a single section in a single chapter to detail every possible contributor to our understanding of time, because time has received great attention in both literature and philosophy. Instead, we concentrate on the major philosophies concerning time, and individual contributors who have helped in our understanding of it.

A History of Time

Eternal Time.   Perhaps the earliest view of time is that of eternal time. Human beings understand that if they live, they will also die. Yet, many religions of the world (Judaism, Christianity, Islam, and Zoroastrianism) believe that physical death is followed by an everlasting life elsewhere—in heaven, hell, or sheol. Other religions (Buddhism) and individuals (e.g., Plato) hold that people have more than one life, and are "reborn in the time flow of life" (Encyclopedia Britannica, 1999, p. 663). Greek philosophers Pythagoras and Empedocles, who lived in the 5th and 6th centuries B.C., claimed they existed in other lives.

The philosophy of an eternal life varies in some degrees from culture to culture and religion to religion. Yet, these philosophies share many tenants, including the notion of continuing life after death (or rebirth), and belief in a supreme deity (God/Yahweh/Allah). Eternal life among many Protestant faiths holds the view that time on Earth is just a dimension we pass to on our way to an eternal life. Protestants believe that God's universal plan provides for eternal life over death, where time is inconsequential.

Eternal time is the oldest philosophical examination of time. Not meant to be scientific, it is built on individual faith and religious beliefs and values. It is part of our individual experience, and something that all human beings struggle to grasp and understand.

Cyclical Time.   Another commonly held philosophy of time concerns its cyclical nature, which differs from time functioning in a linear sense. Cyclical time is most observable in religion, history, and personal life. It is based primarily on recurrences of events, much like the passing of the seasons of the year. Religious ceremonies celebrate past events. Easter and Christmas are the most obvious examples in Western society, but the taking of Holy Communion in many religions is believed by followers to symbolically repeat the Last Supper shared by Christ and the Disciples.

Agriculture lends itself to a tradition of cyclical time. Farmers observed the optimal times of the year for tilling, planting, and harvesting crops. In some cultures, agriculture and religion were interdependent forces believed to provide the food and livelihood necessary for survival. Likewise, viewing the stars in the sky at different seasons signaled different events, and also provided a cyclical perspective.

The notion of rebirth, or reincarnation, represents another form of cyclical time. Rebirth was believed to occur not only in individuals, but also in societies. Aspects of reincarnation vary among different faiths, but essentially most believe that upon death the soul finds a new home in another living being, repeating the life cycle over and over.

Linear Time.   Linear or one-way time posits that time is not a recurring phenomenon, but instead has a definite beginning and perhaps at some point an end. Such a view lies in the belief of an omnipotent creator, with a distinct plan that will someday result in the end of time as known by humans. This perspective has been widely criticized over centuries as being apocalyptic in nature, with no scientific basis for judgment.

Evolutionists, such as Darwin and Democritus, disagreed with the notion of linear time, arguing instead that time is real and has an incredibly long flow of events. The early writings of Democritus trace back to the 5th century B.C., whereas Darwin's more "modern" views sought to illustrate that through natural selection an organism functions within its environment without the presence of some extraneous god.

Contributors to Our Understanding of Time

Throughout history, many individuals have contributed to our understanding and interpretations of time. The following paragraphs summarize the key thinkers, and their views on time.

Aristotle. Aristotle did not study time per se, but he was interested in the study of motion. Aristotle recognized that motion is understood by observing how the location of an object changed. One could talk about "one object moving faster than another" by comparing how much the location of each changed in some interval of time. In Book 4 of the Physics, Aristotle (1999, p. 108) states *"time is the numeration of continuous movement"* (italics added).

Aristotle believed that being at rest was any object's natural state of motion. If an object is in motion, then some agent is responsible for that motion. If the agent stops, then the motion stops. Aristotle's idea that time is perceived through motion failed to recognize that time is independent, and exists as an entity of its own right. Still, it is one of the earliest views of time that exists.

Galileo. Like Aristotle, Galileo did not approach the study of time, but his work and experimentation paved the way for the first principles of relativity, which are related to time. Furthermore, Galileo contradicted Aristotle's notion of a body at rest and the passage of time. Galileo's work was critical in establishing time as a "fundamental measurable quantity ... in the activity of the cosmos" (Davies, 1995, p. 30).

Galileo is credited with the discovery of the basic laws of the pendulum—that its time is independent of the amplitude of the swing. This discovery revolutionized precision clockwork throughout the continent of Europe, and later influenced the work of Sir Isaac Newton.

Newton. In the late 17th century, Newton built on the earlier work of Galileo in establishing the laws of motion, providing a foundation for the mechanical laws of physics. Newton's contribution to the study of time is critically important, in that Newton was able to distinguish "absolute" time from "relative, apparent and common time" (Encyclopedia Britannica, 1999, p. 665). To Newton, time was inherent in the study of motion, because material bodies move along paths that are predictable (over time), subject to the forces that accelerate them.

Davies (1995, p. 31) pointed out that, to Newton, "Time is in its very essence mathematical." For Newton, absolute time represented an ideal scale of time, in which apparent time resulted from the irregularities found in the motion of the Earth. Common time is simply the time that is presently shared. In this sense, Newton's time can be looked at in terms of past and future. Newton's discoveries enabled him to calculate the motion of the moon and other planets, as well as the paths of various types of projectiles and other earthly bodies. In this sense, Newton was the first to bridge the gap between space and time. Newton not only dealt with the theory of motion, but also provided the mathematical tools to measure the phenomenon, leading to the development of calculus. Newton's contributions are numerous, especially in our understanding of scientific theory.

Einstein.   Thanks to Newton, time played a key role in the physical world, establishing the linkage of space and time with reality. It was within this context that the work of Albert Einstein began 2 centuries later. The groundbreaking work of Einstein challenged the Newtonian concept of a universal (absolute) time, leading to Einstein's theory of relativity.

Einstein recognized that time is central to the observer, or, to state it another way, that time is relative. Einstein and his resulting theory of relativity in 1915 brought to the field of physics a concept of time that is flexible and not rigid. As Hawking (1998, p. 23) observed, "The theory of relativity put an end to [Newton's] absolute time." In its simplest form, the theory of relativity posits that the laws of science will be the same for all freely moving observers, despite their speed. Einstein's ideas on relativity revolutionized scientific thought regarding space and time, leading to a new field of study known as *quantum physics.* Time could no longer be thought of in simple terms of past, present, and future.

Hawking.   Toward the end of the 20th century, scholars began to probe deeper into the spacetime continuum brought to the forefront by Newton and Einstein. The idea of a space–time continuum has even manifested itself in popular culture, through science fiction writing and television programs and films like "Star Trek" and "SG-1 (Stargate)." Although many scholars have made salient contributions to the concept of space–time, the work of Stephen W. Hawking identifies him as one of the more influential scholars of the period.

Hawking helped build on the knowledge established in quantum physics to enter into a new realm of thought, theoretical physics. In terms of his contributions to the concept of time, Hawking (1998) observed there are three distinct "arrows" of time. The thermodynamic arrow of time is driven by disorder or entropy. Hawking explained that in any closed system, such as the world, entropy and disorder increase with time—what could be described in lay terms as "Murphy's Law." The psychological arrow of time allows each of us to feel time pass. We remember the past, but we cannot remember the future. The third arrow is what Hawking called the "cosmological arrow of time." It represents "the direction of time in which the universe is expanding rather than contracting" (Hawking, 1998, p. 145).

In his seminal work, *A Brief History of Time* (1998), Hawking detailed the relationship of the three arrows of time in developing a unified theory of physics that could potentially explain the mysteries of the universe and the mysteries of time. Although Hawking's contributions to quantum mechanics and theoretical physics are many, his views on time and its relationship to humans and the universe at large illustrate the rich, historical views on the concept of time from its humble beginnings with Aristotle.

TIME AND MEDIA MARKETS—A LITERATURE REVIEW

Having examined some of the philosophical approaches to time and key individuals who have contributed to our understanding of time as a concept, we now turn to look at how time has been examined in the study of media markets. We use the term *media markets* to encompass a broad orientation to identify the key studies considering the topic of time and media markets.

Time Allocation. Much of the research linking time and media markets involves research examining time allocation in the use of media. Over the years, time allocation has been studied using different phrases, among them *time management, time budgeting,* and *time-shifting,* to name a few.

Studies of time allocation are often grounded in economic theory (DeSerpa, 1971), which approaches time as a limited, scarce resource, built on the premise that there are only 24 hours in a day, 168 hours in a week, and so on. Becker's studies on time allocation (1965, 1976) follow this approach, and although they don't deal solely with media markets, they do approach time allocation for leisure activities, which traditionally encompass media usage.

Some early studies did approach time allocation and media usage. Belson (1961) studied the impact of television in its early development on the purchase and reading of printed material. Smythe (1962) considered time, market, and structural aspects of the media in examining usage from a political economy perspective. Kline (1971) looked at how media usage patterns differ across changes in demographics and lifestyles.

Block (1979) reviewed time allocation in mass communication research by looking at various historical approaches and models regarding time allocation. Block claimed, "The allocation of time has not received the attention that it deserves in contemporary mass communications research" (p. 47), and called for greater collaboration with economic and anthropological approaches to the study of time and media use.

Time Allocation Across Cultures. A limited body of research has examined time allocation across different cultures. Szalai's study (1966) represented one of the earliest works in this area, with its comparative analysis of time allocation, but it contained no direct discussion of media usage. The author continued work in this area with the publication of an edited volume examining time allocation across 12 different countries (Szalai, 1972). Nieto (2000) considered time allocation and media use in a detailed analysis of the Spanish population in one of the more contemporary and richer studies of time and media allocation.

Time as a Variable of Study.   The concept of time is often found as a key variable in different types of research, especially in regards to methodology. Some examples of this type of research include trend studies, which look at patterns of different variables over time (e.g., Greco, 1999); diffusion studies, which consider the impact of new technologies (e.g., cable, VCRs, satellite, Internet) on media usage (Levy, 1981; Lindstrom, 1997; Van den Bulck, 1999; Wirth, 1990); and studies that utilize time-series analysis as a methodological tool (Tharp & Stanley, 1992).

Theoretical Aspects of Time.   An area of research sorely lacking is the consideration of the theoretical aspects of time. Kline (1977) offered the most compelling examination of this topic. In this particular work, Kline reviewed three ways to examine the temporal dimension.

Kline first suggested examining time as a social factor, encompassing two different areas. The first area is time as a resource, which is built on an economic rationale of a finite quality of time. The second conceives of time as a social factor via the meaning time is given. There are several applications possible, including attitudes toward time and their own system of social dynamics.

Second, time can also be studied as a causal link. In this domain, time is usually viewed in a particular setting, or along a sequence of events. The former offers the opportunity to consider patterns among relationships or events, whereas the latter allows researchers the ability to understand the ordering and impact of events.

Kline also detailed how time can be examined as a quantitative relationship. Of critical importance is the level of measurement entailed—whether nominal, ordinal, or interval. Each level offers unique opportunities to investigate time. In evaluating qualitative approaches, Kline distinguished between time as a social process and time as social change. Regardless, a variety of outcomes are possible when considering qualitative aspects of time.

Together, these studies help further our understanding of time and the study of media markets. Still, questions remain regarding the emphasis that researchers place on the concept of time. How has time been examined in scholarly media literature?

THE STUDY OF TIME IN SCHOLARLY MEDIA JOURNALS

To answer this question, we examined the contents of five journals from 1980 to 2000 using the Communication Abstracts online database. The journals selected for study were the *Journal of Broadcasting and Elec-*

tronic Media, Journalism and Mass Communication Quarterly, Journal of Media Economics, Communication Research, and *Journal of Communication.*[2] These five journals are all well known to media researchers, and are considered high-quality journals known for publishing papers related to media industries and markets.

A simple search technique was conducted using the full record of the published article. In this database, the full record consists of the title of the article and the abstract. For each journal search, the single word of *time* was used to analyze the database of articles for each publication. If the word *time* was used in the title or the abstract, it was considered a "hit." The results of the search process are detailed in Table 1.3.

The results are particularly surprising. Of the hundreds of articles published in these five journals between 1980 and 2000, only 25 articles used the word *time* in either the title of the work or the abstract. For example, in the *Journal of Broadcasting and Electronic Media,* of the 13 articles identified, the word *prime-time* was found in 6 of the articles.

These findings suggest that, of the many researchers studying the media, few were either interested in or concerned about the concept of time, even though we have established its relevance and importance to researchers earlier in this chapter. This database search led to another examination, this time focusing on one particular journal.

Of the five journals examined, the *Journal of Media Economics* (JME) is the most likely journal to publish papers directly related to media markets. In this second phase, the first author reviewed the entire list of articles published in JME from 1988 to 2000 using a content analysis. We were curious to learn (a) how many articles used "time" as a variable of study, and (b) how time was examined.

TABLE 1.3
Database Search Results for Selected Journals

Title of Journal	Number of Hits
Journal of Broadcasting and Electronic Media	13
Journalism and Mass Communication Quarterly	6
Journal of Media Economics	3
Communication Research	3
Journal of Communication	0

[2]We acknowledge that using 1980 may seem arbitrary to readers, but the Communication Abstracts electronic database begins at this date. From a theoretical view, as media have expanded and consumed more individual time over the years, it was felt that studies examining time or considering time as a variable of study would most likely be represented during this 20-year span of scholarship.

This detailed analysis of the *Journal of Media Economics* consisted of a total of 171 published articles.[3] Of the 171 published articles, a total of 52 studies (30.4%) used time as a variable of study, operationalized in four different ways. Trend studies (or studies examining patterns over time) were the most popular, followed by media usage (allocation) studies, case studies, and "other" studies (see Table 1.4).

IMPLICATIONS AND CONCLUSIONS

This review of scholarly journals and the detailed analysis of the contents of the *Journal of Media Economics* suggest that researchers have either ignored or perhaps simply overlooked the concept of time as a key variable of study. Where time has been used as a variable of study, its main usage has been in conducting trend analysis over a period of time.

What are the reasons for this lack of attention to such an important topic? We can only speculate on a few possibilities. Perhaps the most obvious reason is that time as a concept of study is simply taken for granted. Because time is not the primary or even secondary reason of interest for conducting research on media markets, the concept tends to be overlooked.

Another possibility is that researchers simply may not be aware of the importance of studying the temporal dimension (something we hope to stimulate with the publication of this text!). Unless one truly considers the importance of time and how the concept might impact the research process, time is likely to be ignored. Historically, only a handful of media researchers have conducted studies related to time. The late F. Gerald Kline was perhaps the most prominent in the United States, and Alfonso Nieto (2000) his counterpart in Spain.

One other possibility, and possibly the most plausible, is that time-based studies are perhaps more challenging to conceptualize and ad-

TABLE 1.4
Time as a Variable of Study in JME, 1988–2000

Types of Studies	Number of Studies
Trend studies	38
Media usage	6
Case studies	2
Other*	4

Other refers to four different topics that could not be collapsed into a single category. The category includes studies on ownership, policy and regulation, time-series analysis, and theatrical release of feature films.

[3]The *Journal of Media Economics* began publication in 1988 as a semi-annual journal. In 1991, it was published three times a year. JME became a quarterly journal in 1994.

minister. For younger academic researchers, the emphasis on publishing—along with the backlog related to actually getting an article in print—force them to focus on short-term projects. Time-based studies, especially using trend data, are often more costly to perform. With limited sources of research funding, researchers tend to take paths of least resistance. Finally, researchers may lack the methodological tools to conduct many time-based studies, whether they involve multivariate analysis (such as time-series analysis) or longitudinal panel designs, which can be complicated to design and analyze.

Clearly, much more can be learned about the concept of time and its application to media markets. These are but a few areas in which we feel new research is warranted. Although there is much to be learned about the temporal dimension and its impact on media markets, the remainder of this book offers some interesting examinations related to the concept of time. In the following chapters, different authors approach the study of time and media markets from very different perspectives. In some chapters, time is the key variable under study, whereas in others it is a contributing variable of study.

This diverse collection of chapters will hopefully encourage other researchers to consider more carefully the concept of time and its application to the study of media markets. By learning more about the concept of time and its importance to media markets, our knowledge grows from both practical and theoretical perspectives.

REFERENCES

Aristotle. (1999). *Physics.* (R. Waterfield, Trans.). New York: Oxford.

Becker, G. S. (1965). A theory of the allocation of time. *Economic Journal, 75,* 493–517.

Becker, G. (1976). *The economic approach to human behavior.* Chicago: University of Chicago Press.

Belson, W. A. (1961). Effects of television on the reading and buying of newspapers and magazines. *Public Opinion Quarterly, 25,* 366–381.

Block, M. P. (1979). Time allocation in mass communication research. In M. J. Voigt & G. J. Hannemann (Eds.), *Progress in communication sciences* (Vol. 1, pp. 29–50). Norwood, NJ: Ablex.

Davies, P. (1995). *About time. Einstein's unfinished revolution.* New York: Simon & Schuster.

DeSerpa, A. C. (1971). A theory of the economics of time. *Economic Journal, 81,* 828–846.

Encyclopedia Britannica, Inc. (1999). *New Encyclopedia Britannica (15th ed.). Volume 28. Macropedia. Knowledge in Depth.* Chicago: Author.

Greco, A. N. (1999). The impact of horizontal mergers and acquisitions on corporate concentration in the U.S. book publishing industry, 1989–1994. *The Journal of Media Economics, 12*(3), 165–180.

Hawking, S. W. (1998). *A brief history of time. From the big bang to black holes.* New York: Bantam.

Kline, F. G. (1971). Media time budgeting as a function of demographics and life style. *Journalism Quarterly, 48,* 211–221.

Kline, F. G. (1977). Time in communication research. In P. M. Hirsch, P. V. Miller, & F. G. Kline, (Eds.), *Strategies for communications research* (pp. 187–204). Beverly Hills, CA: Sage.

Levy, M. (1981). Home video recorders and time shifting. *Journalism Quarterly, 58*(3), 401–405.

Lindstrom, P. B. (1997). The Internet: Nielsen's longitudinal research on behavioral changes in use of this counterintuitive medium. *The Journal of Media Economics, 10*(2), 35–40.

Nieto, A. (2000). *Time and the information market: The case of Spain.* Pamplona: University of Navarra.

Smythe, D. W. (1962). Time, market and space factors in communication economics. *Journalism Quarterly, 39,* 3–14.

Szalai, A. (1966). Trends in comparative time-budget research. *The American Behavioral Scientist, 9*(9), 3–8.

Szalai, A. (1972). *The use of time: Daily activities of urban and suburban populations in twelve countries.* The Hague: Mouton.

Tharp, M., & Stanley, L. (1992). A time series analysis of newspaper profitability by circulation size. *The Journal of Media Economics, 5*(1), 3–12.

U.S. Department of Commerce. (2000). *Statistical abstract of the United States* (120th ed.). Washington, DC: Author.

Van den Bulck, J. (1999). VCR-use and patterns of time shifting and selectivity. *Journal of Broadcasting and Electronic Media, 43*(3), 316–326.

Wirth, M. O. (1990). Cable's impact on over-the-air broadcasting. *The Journal of Media Economics, 3*(2), 39–53.

2

MEDIA AND REPRESENTATIONS
OF TIME[1]

Jacques Durand
(Past Director of the Centre d'études d'opinion, Paris)

The studies made on time budgets show the considerable part that the consumption of media takes in the course of our days. But the effect of media is not restricted to the length devoted to them in our time budget. A television program indeed influences us greatly beyond the time of its broadcasting: Its influence begins as we are intending to view it, and lasts as long as we remember seeing it. We must go farther; the time we spend using media is an occupation like no other; media have their own temporality, and they propose to immerse us in another time. And we may finally wonder if, in the long run, the way we use media doesn't lead to deep changes in the representations we have of the reality of time.

MEDIA AND INDIVIDUAL TIME BUDGETS

The more visible effect of media is the considerable part they occupy in their audiences' time budgets, and this part is growing: In a half-century, the number of movies seen by the average spectator changed from one per week to one or two per day. In 30 years, the number of available television channels went from one to three, and then six, and finally several hundred. TV's broad-

---

[1]For questions, contact: Jacques Durand, 21 Allée des Soudanes, F-78430, Louveciennes, France. E-mail: Jacques.durand19@wanadoo.fr

casting duration, at first limited to a few hours, now covers the whole day. And new media, like the Internet, occupy a greater part of our time.

In France, the population dedicates one fourth of the time they spend in their homes to activities of communication; television represents half of that duration. One fourth of working people devote more than 5 hours per day to communication, and one fourth of nonworking people devote more than 8 hours (Charpin, Forsé, & Périn, 1989). In France, the average daily television viewing time is now nearly 3½ hours (204 minutes), and the average radio listening time is more than 2½ hours (164 minutes).

There are considerable differences among individuals. In 1989, the Médiamat panel indicated that 10% of French people (the "low viewers") watched television on average 8 minutes per day, and that 10% (the "heavy viewers") viewed it 7 hours (Scaglia, 1990). The very short or very long viewings registered by meters may not be real, however, but instead could be the result of panelist or equipment failures. For this reason, Médiamétrie (operator of the French audimeter panel Médiamat) eliminates the viewings that seem too long to be credible (more than 12 hours for a household, more than 9 hours without change of channel for an individual).

The strong constraints that media exert on our time budgets necessarily have great impact on our daily lives. For instance, the greater number of television channels, and the later and later diffusion of their programs, compete with people's sleeping hours. In 10 years, from 1979 to 1989, the number of TV channels in France grew from three to six. Correlatively, the average daily amount of television viewing grew from 128 to 192 minutes. The average sleeping duration remained about the same (passing from 509 to 507 minutes), but the hours of sleeping greatly changed: The proportion of people asleep at 10 P.M. was reduced by half (from 29.3% to 14.5%), and it was doubled at 8 A.M. (from 16.5% to 32.4%; CESP, 1979, 1989). We don't sleep less, but we go to bed later, and we also rise later.

These data may lead us to think that media have a very negative impact on the way people manage their time. The time available for creative activities may be very small. Henry David Thoreau (1967) wrote in his *Journal* that, if you are assigned to work on or create something, you must begin immediately, without being disturbed by your surroundings. There are not many hours in a day; if you spend 2 or 3 hours watching television, you will not have much time for other projects. Eventually, you will arrive at the end of your life, asking yourself why it was so empty.

To remedy this difficulty, Bernard Cache suggested some years ago that television channels be taxed, in order to compensate for the time wasting that they bring about: "This tax may be considered as the compensation of the taking effected by the television system on the time of the television viewers. It may be seen as a compensation of the withdrawal effected on this essential primary good which is time" (Cache, 1989, p. 108).

But we have to take into account the diversity of points of view. For some people, the important thing is to escape from boredom, to find an occupation that allows them to fill their time, and television perfectly meets this need. Other people, in contrast, are overwhelmed by projects; they try to manage their time in a rational way, to do most things quickly and efficiently. To these people, watching television generates "lost time" or at least "expensive time." A 1997 survey indicated that 18% of French people feel that they are bored during their leisure hours (particularly the youngest and the oldest); in contrast, 39% feel that they do not have enough time to accomplish all that they want to do (especially those aged 25 to 55 years, and those with the highest incomes; Donnat, 1998).

Methods were proposed to teach us how to make good use of our time, become conscious of what unnecessarily encumbers it, determine what we wish to do with it, define our objectives in life, and so on (Servan-Schreiber, 2000). In particular, methods were proposed to help us make good use of media. Consider the example of a Cistercian monastery:

> At Soligny, there is only one radio set, one television set and one video recorder. They are here only to allow the brother in charge of the programs to select them, to record them, and to pass them on to the community, if they wish. ... It is not a matter of voluntary reclusion. The world gets through the walls of the monastery, but not through the immediacy of the news, not in the "useless tornado of the urgency." What is cultivated in the convent is another relation with time, a relation which is not constrained, but accepted, calculated. (Tincq, 1998, p. 12)

AUDIENCE MEASURES AND THE STRUCTURE OF TIME

If you want to utilize the results of audience surveys and studies of time budgets, you must take into account the processes used to collect these data. Methods presently used in this field are based on respondents' recollections of their activities the day before. These methods are often criticized because of the risk of errors related to memory: which of us, unexpectedly interrogated, would be able to precisely describe at what moment the day before we watched television or listened to radio, and what channel was on? It is necessary to go farther and analyze the temporal scheme that these methods imply.

These methods actually presuppose that:

- There exists a categorization of time into years, months, weeks, days, hours, minutes, seconds, and that it is universally accepted.
- TV or radio programs are presented precisely within this grid.
- Individuals have at their disposal the instruments (calendar, clock, watch, etc) that allow them to locate themselves on this grid, and that they are always aware of their position.

This fragmentation of time, which is very familiar to us, will seem obvious. But we must remember that it is relatively recent, has not totally eliminated previous fragmentations, and tends to change under the influence of the media themselves.

As Jacques Attali recalled, until the 14th century the day was divided up into 7 hours, not 24 hours. The definition of a universal time, linked to the Greenwich meridian, dates from 1885. The unification of the hour in the whole of France dates from 1891. Watches have been commonly used in France only since the 1930s (Attali, 1982); even as late as 1968, a survey indicated that 17% of French people did not wear any watch.

If we consider the whole world, the agreement on our temporal fragmentation is still less unanimous. The traditional time fragmentations survive in many regions (India, Africa, Muslim countries, etc.; UNESCO, 1975). As Guy Robert, of *Radio France Internationale,* remarked, is it really reasonable to use our familiar questionnaires in these countries, and ask people living these to remember their radio listening on a grid broken down into quarter hours?

It was the media who were responsible for this time fragmentation. Until the 19th century, every town lived at the hours rung out by its belfry, which was adjusted to the sun. The development of the railways required the unification of the hour on the whole French territory, but that was possible only by the use of the telegraph, after 1880. Since 1920, radio (and since 1950, television) allowed the knowledge of the official hour to be spread among the whole population: "The television receiver is the contemporary clock, which regulates the time of daily life" (Perriault, 1989, p. 163).

We should add that, in their historical development, the media imposed on their audiences smaller and smaller time fragments: the year with almanacs, the month or the week with magazines, the day with newspapers, and the minute with radio and television.

Audiovisual media go far beyond displaying the hour; they tend to appropriate the time fragmentation ("it's 9 o'clock on Europe 1"), or even bend it. In France, for a long time the prime time program was called "the 8:30 P.M. program," even if it started at 8:50. Also, in the audience surveys, the respondents refer more to the theoretical time than to the actual time of broadcasting. They will say they began viewing something at 10:00 if the program they viewed was scheduled to begin at 10:00, even if they really tuned in before the program started, or if it began behind schedule. The result is that the audience surveys on television viewing, as opposed to audimetric measures, display an abnormal concentration on round hours (6:00, 7:00, etc.).

The structure of time is imposed by the radio or television program grid, with the same rigor as schedules of work or travel. Interestingly, it often is given a religious connotation:

- "The need to ritualize the measure of time, which was satisfied with the sound of the angelus or of trains, settled later on radio, and now on television news" (Perriault, 1989, p. 155).
- "Television clearly has a religious function, and its appointments, its grid, its jingles give rhythm to the daily and weekly time, like formerly,

in the countryside, the bells of the village, or in monasteries divine offices, from matins to complin[e]" (Debray, 1991, p. 322).

* "Father Di Falco, manager of the magazine *La Vie,* regretted, in February 1991, that the daily communion of French people with the television journal at 8:00 P.M. would become the main religious event of this end of twentieth century" (Mamou, 1991, p. 22).

BEFORE- AND AFTEREFFECTS OF MEDIA EXPOSURES

Eric Berne (1977) showed that the effects of an activity may cover a time segment much greater than its strict duration. It is indeed necessary to take into account the *anticipation* and the *repercussion* effects. Berne defined *anticipation* as "the space of time when a recent event starts to influence the behavior of the individual" (p. 220), and *repercussion* as "the space of time when a past event influences the behavior of the individual" (p. 222). Berne gave as an example the case of a person who had to deliver a half-hour lecture. The person had to admit that this activity perturbed his life during the 5 days prior to the lecture, and also during the 12 days that followed it (p. 220).

The same holds true in respect of the consumption of audiovisual media. The temporal incidence of a program is not limited to the strict duration of its broadcasting. It may also create some pre-and posteffects.

If we learn that in a few days a radio or a television channel intends to broadcast a program that interests us, this program will inscribe itself in our memory, and will interfere with our daily activities. It will come back to our mind insofar as we fear to miss it.

Conversely, a program that had a great impact on us will make a deep impression in our memory, and may linger for many years. For instance, in a recent letter to a magazine, a woman evoked the deep but vague memory she had retained of a broadcast she had listened to a half-century before: "Mrs. B. is trying to locate someone who might remember a rather upsetting radio broadcast—one evening during the year of 1946. We had to wait a couple of days to learn that it was a [play], apparently [done] by Jean Nocher. I would like to read what he or she remembers of that broadcast" (Betton, 2001). This particular program was *Plate-Forme 70 ou L'âge Atomique* by Jean Nocher, and it had been broadcast on February 4, 1946, from 8:45 P.M. to 9:15 P.M. It caused reactions similar to those produced 8 years earlier by Orson Welles' *War of the Worlds* broadcast ("Plate-Forme 70," 1996).

THE TIME INCLUDED INSIDE THE MEDIA

The consumption of any medium takes up a certain amount of time. But, if you want to evaluate the temporal impact of the medium—for example, television—you must add to the amount of time actually spent consuming it, the amount of time its recording encompasses. This amount of time includes the uses that may eventually be made of these recordings in the future. For instance, if you want to measure the television audience, you must take into account videocassette recordings made that the viewers make so they can watch the program at a later time.

As soon as we set aside the books we want to read, the videocassettes we wish to view, the CDs we'd like to hear, and so on, we are stocking at home, on a virtual stage, a definite amount of time. Each one of these books, each one of these cassettes, each one of these CDs represents a certain amount of time that will be required to read, view, or listen to it. In 1997, the French owners of VCRs owned an average of 57 videocassettes (Donnat, 1998); viewing these cassettes would have occupied all their free time for several weeks. Think about it: How much time would fashion designer Karl Lagerfeld need to read the 230,000 books that he claims to own (Belleret, 2001)?

Moreover, the temporal aspect of a media is not limited to the duration of our consumption of it; it lies also in the fact that the media conveys its own temporality. When we watch a movie, we don't use only a part of our available time—we enter into another time. In a way, media makes a hole in the reality of time, and inserts into that hole an imaginary time. In this respect, film and television are similar to music, or some might say even similar to drugs (Winn, 1979).

The analysis of the temporality of media must not be restricted to this duality of times (real time and imaginary time). Etienne Souriau defined eight levels of reality implied by the phenomenon of film: the *afilmic, profilmic, filmographic, filmophanic, ecranic, diegetic, creatorial,* and *spectatorial* realities (Souriau, 1951, 1953). Each of these levels is related to a specific temporality. If we consider the order of a movie's different sequences, they may be shot (profilmic level) in an order different from that in which they are presented on the pellicle (filmographic level). If the projectionist inverts the reels, this order will be different from that in which the sequences appear onscreen (filmophanic level). It may also be different from the chronology of the plot of the movie (diegetic level), if flashbacks are included in the scenario. Finally, the filmgoer may not understand this chronology (spectatoriel level).

ATTITUDES TOWARDS TIME

It is well known that the uses of media, and especially of audiovisual media, are directly related to time. Audience studies and time-budget surveys measure how people consume media in the course of their days. But the relation between media and time may be analyzed at another level, that of representations. There may indeed be a link between our conception of time and the way we use media:

- Uses of media may differ, according to the conceptions of time adopted by the audiences. Because of these attitudes, individuals may tend to choose some media instead of others, and will use them in different ways.

- Particular conceptions of time may be implicit in media. Whether from their structural modalities or their contents, media may imply some ideas about time.
- Media may influence the representations of time among audiences. Daily use of specific media may, over time, modify attitudes of audiences about time.

There may exist several attitudes toward time, which differ by the degree of reality they allocate to the past, the present, and the future. However, these attitudes don't necessarily belong to different individuals: Each of us may, according to the moment, go from one to another.

The first attitude pretends strictly to take into account our immediate experience. It considers that the *present* is the only reality. Neither the past nor the future exists, apart from our representation. As Saint Augustine said (Saint Augustine, 1955), "The past doesn't exist anymore, and the future doesn't exist yet" (*"Praeteritum jam non est, et futurum nondum est"*).

You can even assume that the past has never existed. "There is no logical impossibility to assume that the world began five minutes ago, with all men remembering a completely unreal past" (Bertrand Russell, quoted in Ruyer, 1966, p. 114).

The second conception is that of a *linear time*. According to this idea, time is, like space, one of the dimensions of the universe. Events are located along the axis of time, which can be represented by a straight line (see Fig. 2.1).

According to this conception, the past and the future have the same degree of reality. Like the past, the future is unique. The fact that we don't know it results from the orientation of our consciousness, not from its nonexistence or the plurality of possible futures. The whole time is given: Time doesn't go by; instead, we move along it, progressively discovering future realities. This conception is the one we find in relativistic physics: "For us, convinced physicists, the distinctions between the past, the present and the future are only an illusion, even if it is tenacious" (Albert Einstein, quoted by Costa de Beauregard, 1963, p. 8). Several positions implicitly refer to this conception of the linearity of time. Examples include each time the future is considered as definite, predetermined, or ineluctable, or in the case of the theology of predestination, laplacian determinism, predictions and prophecies (e.g., Nostradamus), premonitory dreams described by parapsychologists (Dunne, 1927), or time travels imagined by science-fiction writers (e.g., *The Time Machine,* by H. G. Wells). However, this conception seems difficult to accept for living beings: Their thoughts, their actions, and their

TIME

PAST   PRESENT   FUTURE

FIG. 2.1.   Linear Time Conception.

existences suppose that the future is open, not predetermined. Such a conception can appear to them only as an improper extension towards the future of the uniqueness of the past.

The third conception seems to be more acceptable, that of *divergent* time (see Fig. 2.2). At each moment of time, we are facing a plurality of possibilities; only one finally becomes real. Past history results from a succession of alternatives. The future is not fixed; instead, it is open to our actions. But we will then ask what degree of reality must be attached to each of these possibilities, for the past as well for the future. Some people have tried to imagine what our present would be like if a particular event had not happened, or if it had happened differently (Lesourne, 2001).

A frequently assumed solution considers that the past has a linear structure, and the future has a divergent one (Gardies, 1975). The past is unique; its reality is definitely established; we can know it, but we can't act on it anymore. In contrast, the future is not yet fixed, it is open to our actions. Between the past and the future, the present occupies a determinant position, because it is the moment of the transition from multiple to unique, from virtual to real.

It seems that the common perception of time is a little more complex, and that one particular moment—the day we were born—plays an important role. We readily believe that the future is not predetermined, that it offers us a plurality of possibilities, and that our action can reorientate it. With regard to the past that we have already lived, it is easy for us to think that it has also a divergent structure—that it could have been different. We can imagine the other directions that our life could have taken; we can regret the misfortunes we have suffered, and the errors we have made. However, when considering an earlier past, prior to our birth, it is difficult for us to realize that the sequence of events should have been different, and it is particularly difficult for us to imagine what it would have meant not to be born.

These attitudes toward time may be related to the consumption of media. Surveys effectively show that individuals who use different media have different attitudes concerning time. For example, at the beginning of the 1980s a survey conducted by the Centre d'Etude des Supports de Publicité (CESP) compared attitudes toward time among readers of Parisian daily newspapers. The survey found that 27.5% of the readers of popular news-

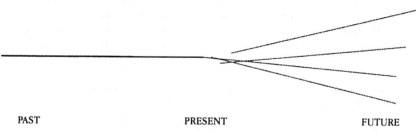

PAST   PRESENT   FUTURE

FIG. 2.2. Divergent time conception.

papers (*France-Soir, Le Parisien, L'Humanité, L'Equipe*) agreed with the statement "I often regret the good old times," compared to only 10.3% of the readers of elitist newspapers (*L'Aurore, Le Monde, Le Figaro, Le Matin, La Croix*; CESP, 1980–1983).

LIVE BROADCASTING AND PERCEPTION OF PRESENT

Radio and television make possible the direct transmission of events, something that other media, such as the press and cinema, are not capable of doing. Yet, this situation is not new. The direct relation is the norm for shows (e.g., theater, concerts, sports) and the telephone. According to the terminology of Souriau (1951, 1953), direct is the transmission coincidence of *afilmic* time, *diegetic* time, and *ecranic* time.

The main advantage of live broadcasting is to give a greater impression of reality and life, which allows us to experience more intensely, together with a large audience, an event that is both present in time and distant in space. The most momentous broadcasts in the history of television have been the live transmission, all over the world, of events such as the coronation of the Queen Elizabeth II on June 2, 1953; Neil Armstrong's walk on the moon on July 20, 1969; or the terrorist attacks on September 11, 2001.

The other advantage of live broadcasting lies in its unpredictability. For example, this is the appeal of the broadcasting of live sport events. The outcome is uncertain, and at any time something unexpected may occur.

For a live broadcast to have impact on the television viewer, the viewer must be aware of the fact that it is live. Surveys indicate that even children can and do master this technical process:

> When he sees a match broadcasted live, the child [10 to 11 years old] knows that the action filmed by the camera is unfolding at the moment when he sees it. The duration lived by the players is the same as the one lived by the viewer. Every technical modification on the time of the show, such as the slow-motion play-back of a goal, is seen as an action undertaken by television technicians which is independent from the process of the match. (Pierre et al., 1982, p. 147)

In the past, live broadcasting gave rise to much analysis, particularly during the Gulf War. The initial evaluations were positive. For the first time, one could "see a war live on all the television screens of the world" (L.-W., 1991, p. 28), and everyone admired the performance of CNN. Shortly afterwards, however, the judgments became more critical. Commentators like Paul Virilio (1991) or Dominique Wolton (1991) criticized "live information" as being a "show information," preventing the journalists from thinking, having "an uncontrollable psychological impact on the population," and having a dangerous influence on the decisions of those actually running the war.

A similar problem also appeared in the financial field. The instantaneous link between national markets was considered responsible for the excessive reactions of markets during times of crisis.

The question of live broadcasting may also come up in the field of audience measurement: Some companies, like Nielsen and Arbitron in the United States and Telemetric in France, installed systems to instantaneously measure a broadcast's audience. But could instantaneous audience measurements disturb how channels are run? We must remember that, in the United Kingdom, for a long time the BBC has opposed even daily results, because it feels that such data—and reactions to them—might place too great a constraint on its own programming. A cartoon published many years ago showed an orchestra playing in a radio studio, where a dial displayed how much of an audience was tuning in. At one point the conductor put down his baton and told the musicians, "There is no point in playing any further, nobody is listening to us anymore."

NEWSPAPERS AND THE IMAGE OF THE PAST

The use of the newspaper by its readers is closely connected to the readers' attitude toward time, particularly with the interest he or she takes in past events. Some people, who give primacy to the present, will consider a newspaper to be an object of ephemeral consumption, which they will throw away right after reading it. In a pinch, they will take it as a documentation element, keep it as long it is useful, and throw it away when they judge it to be out of date. In contrast, other people, who take a greater interest to the past, will tend to keep newspapers and reviews, or at least some articles.

Some people keep newspapers as a source of information on past events, such as those of historical significance (e.g., a declaration of war, an armistice, the death of a famous person, etc.). The choice of documents is made according to how significant a person finds the event, and the degree of confidence he or she puts in the different newspapers. (This attitude assumes that the newspapers give an exact description of the intriguing event.)

For other people, a newspaper is of interest if it expresses a certain opinion. Even if it gives a distorted view of the facts, it retains historical interest, because it may convey reactions to opinions about these facts; in fact, it may also influence those opinions. We go from the history of events to the history of the representation of events. The criterion of selection here is not the exactness of the information, but the fact that the newspaper clearly expresses a trend of the opinion, or that it had a great influence over it.

Still others may consider a newspaper to be an object having a historical interest in itself, whatever its content. The history of which it keeps some traces is the history of the press itself. The newspaper thus becomes an object of collection. For such readers, every newspaper, whatever it is, deserves to be kept. The interest of a particular issue depends only on its rarity.

Finally, for some people a newspaper may be a means to nostalgically evoke the past. This kind of reading is the one we adopt if we accidentally find a forgotten newspaper. The newspaper here plays the same function as old songs or old photographs—it is an instrument with to play with time, but it forgets all that has been fabricated and contingent on those objects.

Surveys about French press audiences have frequently shown that saving articles is a relatively common practice. In 1963, 58% of the readers of regional newspapers declared that they occasionally found in the newspaper something that they wished to keep. In 1975, 44% of the readers of magazines said that they often or from time to time cut articles out of those magazines (Durand, 1981). In 1980, 68% of the population and 80% of newspaper readers of said that they occasionally cut articles or photographs out of magazines (CESP, 1980–1983).

But the decision to keep a newspaper results not only from the free choice of the reader, sometimes readers are subtly pressured to do so. For example, before the second war, a magazine like *L'Illustration* was presented as "the magazine you must keep" because of the tone of the articles, the quality of the paper and illustrations, the number of pages, the title pages, and the tables of contents. Other publications explicitly offer reprints of past issues: A reader will then be able to buy at a much higher price the facsimile of an issue he or she threw away 20 years ago.

The structure of the newspaper itself implies a certain idea of time. Every day, the newspaper brings us information on events unexpected and unforeseen. It tells us, among all the possible events, which came true, and as such it belongs to the conception of the divergent time. But every day it provides the information, however important or new, in an identical frame (structure, makeup, graphics, etc.), giving the image of an eternal present. When kept in volumes on library shelves, newspapers give us access to a single and unchanging past, and it is the only way of access to this particular portrayal of the past.

PRESENCE OF THE PAST IN THE VISUAL MEDIA

The thoughts presented earlier about the live broadcasting of events on television might let us forget another major fact, that audiovisual media essentially broadcast images of a more or less distant past. In the common representation, the past has two characteristics: It is both unchanging and inaccessible. But here, the audiovisual media create a considerable mutation. Writing or drawing may give only an approximate evocation of the past. Photographic and phonographic techniques allow a literal recording. There is here, as shown by Marc Ferro, new material for the historian (Ferro, 1977). But it is, again, the instrument of a deep questioning of our conception of time.

As André Bazin said, the cinema "realizes the paradox of an objective past, of a memory external to our consciousness. It is a machine to find again the time in order to better lose it" (Bazin, 1958, p. 41). Gaston Berger was ironic about "this quite curious, and yet very spread, belief considering time like a reservoir of images, into which all the present moments would fall, and in which all that has been would stay" (Berger, 1964, p. 137). But don't the audiovisual media precisely constitute such a reservoir of images? They can therefore substantiate the idea that the past has not disappeared, because we keep a visual trace of it.

Whereas 40 or 50 years ago, on Saturday nights people were interested only in new movies and living actors, audiovisual media now broadcast repetitively past works. Specialized channels have been created to exploit this market of nostalgia, and the development of video recording has reinforced this trend.

Until recently, the common fate of humans, after they die, was to be rapidly forgotten: "There is no durable memory, either of the wise, or of the fool; and from the following days they are both forgotten" (*Ecclesiastes,* 2:16). But dead actors today have this particular privilege of periodically coming back in front of us, unchanged, at the different ages of their lives. Surveys show the public's remaining deep attachment to actors who have been dead for many years, like James Dean, Humphrey Bogart, or Marilyn Monroe.

Audiovisual media create new relations with the past. Out of this results a deep change in our relation with time, and particularly in our representation of death. Because it allows us to keep the pictures of dead people, photography takes its place in what Freud called "the work of mourning" and replaces the traditional funeral rites (Robert Castel, in Bourdieu, 1965).

In the case of television programs, the relation with the past may be relatively complex. One program may actually refer to several levels of time simultaneously. If, for instance, a channel broadcasts the movie *Senso* by Visconti, which evokes a performance of an opera by Verdi (*Il Trovatore*), we can find in it the superposition of six temporal levels:

- The date on which this channel is broadcasting the film (*filmophanic* time: now).
- The date when we watched this movie for the first time (*spectatorial* time).
- The date of the realization of the movie (*profilmic* time: 1954).
- The time at which the story related by the movie takes place (*diegetic* time: 1866).
- The date that Verdi created the opera (second *profilmic* time: 1853).
- The time when the story related by the opera takes place (second *diegetic* time: 15th century).

This description is not academic. According to the objectives of our research, we will choose one of these temporal levels. But the TV viewer will also be able, depending on his or her interests and present feeling, to pass from one point of view to the other.

TELEVISUAL FICTION: AN IMAGE OF THE FUTURE

Fictional programs frequently send us to the past. However, by their unfolding, they also imply a certain vision of the future. The very principle of these programs that they are built on a succession of surprises and uncertainties, which are gradually solved, to conduct to a more or less unexpected dénouement.

At a particular time of the story, you may wonder what will be the outcome of these events. The points of view, in this respect, are various. The narrator obviously knows the whole unfolding of the story, until its end. In contrast, the character who lives this story, on the diegetic level, is supposed not to know it (as is the TV viewer, too, if he or she is seeing the program for the first time).

In order to show this diversity of points of view about future, we analyzed how a TV magazine presents the programs scheduled for the coming week. The study concerned the magazine *Télé-Poche* during the month of June 1991 (Durand, 1996).

In such a magazine, the listing about a fictional program (movie or TV film) is often illustrated with a picture taken from the program, and accompanied by a short caption. Each of these pictures illustrates a particular moment in the progression of the film; The picture formulates this moment in the present tense. In contrast, the caption that goes together with the picture subtly plays with the tenses. Some captions are written in the *present* tense, and they directly refer to the scene represented in the photography: "Laugel questions Sophie." Others are written in the *past* tense, and they evoke previous episodes of the story: "After the attack on the ship, which led to its sinking, Angélique finds herself in an unfortunate position." However, the most interesting eventuality is when the text is formulated in the *future* tense. Several cases must be distinguished here.

In a first case, the text stresses on the uncertainty of the future, adopting the point of view of the characters: "Elena hopes that, one day, Roger will relinquish his silence, and will interact with her more." In a second case, the uncertainty of the future, which affects the character, is also attributed to the reader, who is considered to be unaware of the continuation of the story: "Will Woody Wilkins be able to shield beautiful Natalia from her pursuers?" Finally, in a third case, the text clears up the uncertainty and tells the reader what will happen after the scene that is shown in the picture: "The holidays of Mr. Eloi and of his dear wife will not go on as expected."

Three categories of persons intervene in these texts, and each has a different perception of time:

- The characters of the story only have knowledge of their present and their past; they don't know what their future will be. They may think that this future remains open, and that it partly depends on their actions.
- The magazine writer completely knows the past, present, and future of the characters; for him or her, their future is completely determined.
- The reader has the same perception of time as the writer, if he or she has already seen the film presented. If not, the reader doesn't know what will happen to the characters, but realizes that their future is closed.

One is entitled to wonder whether repeated viewing of fictional programs cannot influence the perception that the TV viewer has of his or her
real life. When continuously watching stories whose development they
know is predetermined, don't TV viewers risk thinking that their own lives
are the same—that their destiny is already written somewhere, and that
some God knows it?

CONCLUSION

What image of time is, explicitly or implicitly, conveyed by media? In common use, time has two characteristics: it is irreversible and divergent. To say
that time is irreversible means that it always flows in the same direction, that
it takes us with it, and that we cannot go back. If time is divergent, it means
that the event that occurs is only one among the set of all the events that
could have occurred; from the present moment there are a multitude of
possibilities, and our action may exercise some influence over the choice
among these possibilities.

Media present us with a universe in which temporal structures are different from our daily perception—a universe where time is neither irreversible nor divergent.

Media deny the irreversibility of time. This is obvious with the press,
which gives us a means to find a trace of past events. But it is still more obvious with audiovisual media, which chaotically present us with past periods,
and which let the deceased live again.

Audiovisual media deny the divergence of time. They tell us stories with a
predetermined course. The TV viewer may or may not know the end of the
story, but he or she knows that this story is already written, and that the apparent liberty of the characters is only an illusion.

Many researchers have questioned the effects of the media. They have
wondered whether these could change any political choices, or incite people to violent behaviors. However, one may ask another question, and wonder if the daily consumption of press, television, and radio, in the long run,
may not influence the way in which readers, listeners, and viewers imagine
what time is, the way they manage the development of their everyday lives,
and the meaning they give to the course of their lives.

REFERENCES[2]

Attali, J. (1982). *Histoires du temps* [History of time]. Paris: Arthème Fayard.
Barthes, R. (1980). *La chambre claire—Note sur la photographie* [Camera lucida].
    Paris: Cahiers du cinéma/Gallimard/Seuil.
Bazin, A. (1958). *Qu'est-ce que le cinéma?* [What is cinema?] (Vol. 1). Paris: Edi-
    tions du Cerf.
Belleret, R. (2001, 21 March). Citizen Karl. *Le Monde,* p. 18.

---

[2]Complementary information may be found on my website: http://perso.wanadoo.fr/
jacques.durand/Index.htm

Berger, G. (1964). *Phénoménologie du temps et prospective* [Phenomenology of time and prospective]. Paris: Presses Universitaires de France.

Berne, E. (1977). *Que dites-vous après avoir dit bonjour* [What do you say after you say hello]. Paris: Tchou.

Betton, A. (2001, November–December). *L'Echo d'Aujourd'hui*. Courrier des lecteurs, p. 63.

Bourdieu, P. (1965). *Un art moyen—Essai sur les usages sociaux de la photographie* [Photography—A middle-brow art]. Paris: Editions de Minuit.

Cache, B. (1989, April–June). Rawls regarde la télévision [Rawls watches television]. *Médias Pouvoirs*, p. 102–108.

Centre d'Etude des Supports de Publicité (CESP). (1979). *Etude sur l'emploi du temps et les activités des personnes* [Survey about time budget and activities]. Paris: Author.

Centre d'Etude des Supports de Publicité (CESP). (1980–1983). *Etude expérimentale média contexte* (2 vol.) [Experimental study about the context of media]. Paris: Author.

Centre d'Etude des Supports de Publicité (CESP). (1991–1992). *Etude budget-temps multi-médias* [Time budget and multimedia survey]. Paris: Author.

Charpin, F., Forsé, M., & Périn, P. (1989). Temps et budget de la communication au domicile. *Observations et diagnostics économiques, 27,* 157–176.

Costa de Beauregard, O. (1963). *Le second principe de la science du temps.* Paris: Editions du Seuil.

Debray, R. (1991). *Cours de médiologie générale* [Course of general mediology]. Paris: Gallimard.

Donnat, O. (Ministère de la Culture et de la Communication). (1998). *Les pratiques culturelles des Français—enquête 1997* [The cultural activities of French population—1997 survey]. Paris: La Documentation Française.

Dunne, J. W. (1927). *An experiment with time.* London: Faber and Faber.

Durand, J. (1981). La communication et le temps. In *Les formes de la communication* (pp. 95–118). Paris: Dunod.

Durand, J. (1996). La représentation du temps dans les médias audiovisuels [Representations of time in audiovisual media]. *Communication et langages, 108,* 32–44.

Ferro, M. (1977). *Cinéma et histoire* [Cinema and history]. Paris: Denoël/Gonthier.

Gardies, J.-L. (1975). *La logique du temps* [The logic of time]. Paris: Presses Universitaires de France.

Lesourne, J. (2001). *Ces avenirs qui n'ont pas eu lieu* [These futures which didn't take place]. Paris: Odile Jacob.

L.-W., A. (1991, January 18). Une nuit de direct sans image avec CNN. *Libération*, p. 28.

Mamou, Y. (1991). *C'est la faute aux medias—Essai sur la fabrication de l'information.* Paris, Payot.

Perriault, J. (1989). *La logique de l'usage* [The logic of usage]. Paris: Flammarion.

Pierre, E., Chaguiboff, J., & Chapelain, B. (1982). *Les nouveaux téléspectateurs de 9 à 18 ans* [The new televiewers of ages 9 to 18]. Paris: Flammarion.

"Plate-forme 70": Trente minutes d'angoisse. (1996). *Cahiers d'histoire de la radiodiffusion, 50,* 52–54.

Ruyer, R. (1966). *Paradoxes de la conscience et limites de l'automatisme* [Paradoxes of consciousness and the limits of automatism]. Paris: Albin Michel.

Saint Augustine. (1955). *Confessions.* Livre II, § XIV, p. 283. Paris: Club du livre religieux.

Scaglia, D. et al. (1990). *Médiamat 1989—le livre de l'audience* [The book of audience]. Paris: Médiametrie.

Servan-Schreiber, J.-L. (2000). *Le nouvel art du temps* [The art of time]. Paris: Albin Michel.

Souriau, E. (1951, May). La structure de l'univers filmique et le vocabulaire de la filmologie [The structure of filmic universe and the vocabulary of filmology]. *Revue internationale de filmologie* (Tome II), pp. 231–240.

Souriau, E. (1953). Preface. In *L'univers filmique* (pp. 5–10). Paris: Flammarion.

Thoreau, H. D. (1967). *Un philosophe dans les bois, pages de journal 1837-61* [A philosoph in the woods, pages of journal 1837–61, traduction française] (R. Michaud & S. David, Trans.). Paris: Editions Seghers.

Tincq, H. (1998, March 28). Les aigles du Bon Dieu, *Le Monde*, p. 12.

UNESCO. (1975). *Les cultures et le temps* [Cultures and time]. Paris: Payot/Author.

Virilio, P. (1991, January 23). L'émotion du direct tue la réflexion. *Télérama*, p. 14.

Winn, M. (1979). *TV, drogue* [The plug-in drug]. Paris: Fleurus.

Wolton, D. (1991, January 24). L'information spectacle. *Le Monde*, p. 2.

3

TIME AS A NICHE DIMENSION: COMPETITION
BETWEEN THE INTERNET AND TELEVISION[1]

Daniel G. McDonald
John W. Dimmick
The Ohio State University

The use of time in leisure has been a concern in the social science literature throughout the past century (e.g., Gulick, 1909; Sorokin & Berger, 1939). A primary concern among these studies has been the time spent in mass and interpersonal communication (Edwards, 1915; Graney & Graney, 1974; Gulick, 1909; Hudson, 1951; Kline, 1971; Sweetser, 1955). Historically, new media innovations have reduced time spent with other media. For example, time displacement on traveling performances was recorded for movies and radio (Edwards, 1915; Gulick, 1909; Hurley, 1937; Jones, 1922) whereas movies also displaced time spent with books (Herzog, 1961; Hurley, 1937). From vaudeville through motion pictures, comic books, radio, television, video games, and the Internet, the 20th century witnessed an inexorable march of new media, communication, and entertainment forces, each usurping time from other activities, and each generating some degree of concern

[1]The authors are Professor and Associate Professor, respectively, in the School of Journalism and Communication at the Ohio State University, 3080 Derby Hall, 154 North Oval Mall, Columbus, OH 43210. We would like to thank Dr. Paul Lavrakas and the staff of the Survey Research Center in the College of Social and Behavioral Sciences at the Ohio State University for making the BSP data available for analysis.

over the volume of time being spent on the new medium and from where that time was coming. Although there is some evidence that new media may displace sleeping, eating, social activities, or schoolwork (Cunningham & Walsh, 1958; Hurley, 1937; Swanson & Jones, 1951; Sweetser, 1955), the bulk of the literature suggests that new communications media should have their greatest displacement effects on older communications media because of their functional similarity (Katz, Gurevitch, & Haas, 1973; Ogburn, 1933).

Some of the of the earliest reports of displacement effects of new media were by Zangwill (1905), who documented how vaudeville was destroying multiple-act plays. A few years later, the new medium of motion pictures was "destroying the penny arcade." An article in *The Outlook* suggested that the primary reason for the destruction was that the public had found that, for only a nickel, they could spend about an hour in the movie theater whereas the penny arcade offered a much shorter time for the money (Anonymous, 1912). The article noted that during the previous few years, the number of penny arcades in New York City had declined from 50 to about 10.

By the late 1920s, it was becoming clear that, in small towns, time spent in vaudeville had superceded time spent in dramatic performances (Lynd & Lynd, 1929). In less than a decade, the two newer media, radio and motion pictures, had displaced vaudeville (Lynd & Lynd, 1937).

A few decades later, diffusion of television in the United States occurred at a phenomenal rate, and displacement of time spent with radio was well documented (Bogart, 1957; Cunningham & Walsh, 1958; Hudson, 1951; Swanson & Jones, 1951). The displacement of radio by television had far-reaching effects on the content and structure of the entire radio industry (Sterling & Kittross, 1978).

The growth of the Internet is one of the current media success stories, rivaling the diffusion of television in its rate of adoption. According to a recent study done by Stanford University's Institute for the Quantitative Study of Society, 55% of a national sample of Americans now have access to the Internet (Markoff, 2000). The same study found that about half of those with Internet access were online from 1 to 5 hours a week, 22% used the Internet 5 to 10 hours a week, whereas a further 14% were online more than 10 hours a week. Research by A. C. Nielsen (personal communication to the senior author) indicates that although TV viewing per week increased 16 minutes between 1997 and 2000, time spent on computers between September 1999 and June 2000 increased by 1 hour and 31 minutes. These data suggest that time spent on the Internet may be having an impact on time spent with other media of communication.

The Stanford study measured the impact of the Internet on other media in the only way possible in a single cross-sectional study, by asking respondents who were online 5 or more hours a week whether they had "increased," "decreased," or "remained unchanged" in the amount of time they spent with the traditional media. Using this simple measure, 59% of respondents who were online 5 or more hours per week reported using TV less, and 34% spent less time reading newspapers. The decrement for TV was the single largest impact on another medium recorded in the study (Markoff, 2000).

Similarly, a study by Robinson and Godbey (1997) found that estimates of time spent "yesterday" with traditional media changed between 1994 and 1995, dropping an average of 30 minutes per person. Most of that time (18 minutes) was associated with declining television time.

Although there have been extensive studies of the impact on older media of time spent with a new medium, few studies of the Internet or earlier media have used multivariate procedures, and very few have employed multiple time points in their research designs. The purpose of this chapter is to assess the impact of the Internet on time spent with television using data from 36 independent surveys conducted over a 3-year period. A second objective is to locate the variables most strongly related to the Internet's impact on TV time.

Niche Theory and TV Time

In the language of niche theory, the decrement in TV time observed in the Stanford study, caused by the introduction of the new medium—the Internet—is termed *displacement.* The theory of the niche (Dimmick, 1993; Dimmick & Rothenbuhler, 1984a, 1984b) begins with the proposition that media compete for limited resources. Any two media are in a situation of competition if they use the same resources. One resource for which all media compete is consumer time and attention. All media use requires an expenditure of time. In fact, as some economists have pointed out, all consumption requires expenditures of time. For example, Block (1979) observed, "Consumption involves both the time necessary to consume the goods, as well as the goods themselves" (p. 32). The economic consequences of time spent with the media were recognized decades ago by Kline (1977).

Fig. 3.1 provides a simple depiction of the resources used by media organizations and industries, and their relationship to time spent with media. The most basic and important resources on niche dimensions are the gratification utilities. All media satisfy gratification utilities within particular domains (e.g., news, entertainment, interaction). For studies of gratification utilities, see Albarran and Dimmick (1993), Dimmick (1993), and Dimmick, Kline, and Stafford (2000). As Fig. 3.1 shows, gratification results in consumer spending and in time spent with various media that is then sold to advertisers. This is the manner in which consumer time acquires economic value for media organizations and industries. In the case of commercial television, advertisers buy access to audiences on the basis of program ratings, which are the indexes of consumer time spent with the medium. A decrease in time spent therefore affects the ratings and, hence, the prices charged by television networks and stations. Absent any ability to raise prices, a displacement in time spent with TV will result in lower revenues for networks and stations.

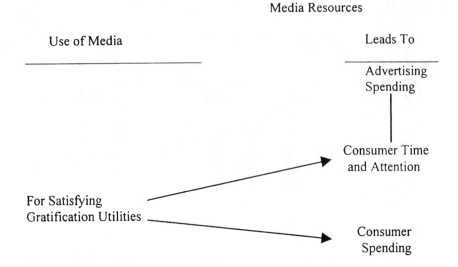

FIG. 3.1.   Relationships among niche dimensions.

HYPOTHESES ABOUT TIME AND THE INTERNET

Americans currently spend more time watching television than any other lei-sure time activity except sleeping (Robinson & Godbey, 1997). As the litera-ture reviewed earlier demonstrates, when the computer enters the household (also the abode of the TV set), there are substantial historical pre-cedents for expecting displacement of TV time. A study by Find/SVP (1997) found that 35% of people who used the internet reported a decline in televi-sion use. However, self-reports of "more," "less," or "about the same" amount of time spent with television do not provide an estimate of the mag-nitude of the effect. The study reported here assesses the extent to which television time (measured in hours and minutes) has declined over time in relation to computers, Internet adoption, and additional control and mediat-ing variables.

Hypothesis 1: During the past 3 years of Internet diffusion, home computer adoption will have resulted in a reduction of time spent watching television.

Both television and the Internet offer diverse content in the realms of in-formation and entertainment so that, in many respects, the two media may qualify as functional alternatives at the level of gratification utilities. The competitive advantage of the Internet over TV is that it offers a great many

33

more possibilities for entertainment and information or gratification opportunities (see Dimmick, 1993, for an explanation of this term). In addition, through e-mail and chat rooms, the Internet provides possibilities for interaction with other people.

> *Hypothesis 2*: During the past 3 years of Internet diffusion, adoption of Internet access for the home computer will have resulted in a reduction of time spent watching television.

There are also good reasons for believing that displacement of TV time by the Internet and the computer will be strongest among the younger age cohort. In the cases of radio (Kirkpatrick, 1933; Lumley, 1934) and television (Swanson & Jones, 1951), diffusion was associated with both higher income and being younger. In addition, studies of aspects of Internet use also show an association with age. A study of e-mail users by Dimmick, Kline, and Stafford (2000), as well as unpublished data collected by Dimmick on the use of online news, shows that Internet users are younger and have higher incomes and educational attainment.

> *Hypothesis 3*: The impact of computers and the Internet on time spent viewing television will be strongest among younger adults after imposing controls for demographic and seasonality variables.

DESCRIPTION OF DATA COLLECTION

The data to test the three hypotheses were drawn from the Buckeye State Poll (BSP) for a 3-year period from November 1996 to October 1999. The Buckeye State Poll is a monthly telephone survey conducted by the Survey Research Center at Ohio State University using a probability sample of residents of the state of Ohio. Respondents are equally distributed across the state of Ohio. For each of the 36 surveys, a computer-generated sample of phone numbers was used to reach each household whether the number was listed or unlisted. Within each household, one English-speaking adult was selected by a random procedure to be a respondent. Up to 10 contact attempts were made to interview the respondent in each household. Sampling error for the 36 surveys is in the area of 3.5%. In all, the data used in this chapter cover 36 monthly surveys with an average sample size of 675 respondents and a total sample size of 22,851 respondents.

In addition to a number of demographic variables such as age, income, education, and number of children in the household, each of the 36 surveys asked respondents whether the household had cable or satellite TV, the average number of hours and minutes that the respondents watched TV daily, whether the home was equipped with a computer, and whether the household had Internet access. A secondary analysis of these variables was used to test the three hypotheses.

RESULTS OF THE ANALYSES

Correlations for the major study variables are presented as Table 3.1. All but four of the correlations in the table are significant at $p < .05$. Three of the four nonsignificant values are associated with the time of the survey (as measured by a simple numbering from 1 to 36), suggesting that there are few trends in the data associated with time.

Two trends that are clearly evident in the data are among the primary independent variables in our study—diffusion of home computers and diffusion of Internet access in the sampled households. The proportion of households with computers and the proportion with Internet access both increased during the 36 months under study. The correlation between time of study and whether or not the household had a computer is .091, and for time of study and Internet households it is .170.

Fig. 3.2 illustrates the diffusion of computers and the Internet graphically by plotting the diffusion aggregated by survey month. The two form nearly parallel lines, with the percentages increasing over time, suggesting that the rate of diffusion is nearly identical, but the original level of diffusion is higher for computers, consistent with the idea that computer diffusion began earlier than Internet diffusion.

The first hypothesis is that time spent with television declines in association with home computer diffusion. The second is that a similar but additive phenomenon should be observed for Internet diffusion. These relationships are graphed in Fig. 3.3, where the means for each variable are plotted for each survey month. Although there is considerable sampling variation for these measures from month to month, the figure would appear to indicate support for both hypotheses. Individuals who live in households in which there is no computer spend the most time with television; those with computers spend less time, and those with computers and the Internet spend the lowest amount of time with television.

Despite what would appear to be a clear effect of diffusion in this visual presentation (Fig. 3.3), it is impossible to conclude from these data that other variables, such as education and income, are not causing these changes. As described earlier, there is a long history suggesting that education and income levels are important in understanding the diffusion of new media and, hence, it is necessary to control for these other variables.

Table 3.2 provides the results of the second step in evaluating the hypotheses, a multiple regression analysis in which time spent with television is the dependent variable and a number of factors known to be associated with TV time are used as independent variables. The table provides information that is highly consistent with previous literature on the subject that stretches back to the 1950s (Cunningham & Walsh, 1958; Kline, 1977). No consistent upward or downward linear trend in television time can be seen in the data (the survey time point is statistically nonsignificant in predicting TV time). In this analysis, as well as the later regression analyses, the Durbin-Watson test indicates that there is no significant autocorrelation. In

TABLE 3.1

Correlation Coefficients for Major Study Variables

	1	2	3	4	5	6	7	8	9	10	11
1. TV time	—										
2. Age	.211	—									
3. Income	-.283	-.133	—								
4. Education	-.253	-.092	.372	—							
5. Adults in household	-.059	-.169	.266	-.017	—						
6. Children in household	-.136	-.348	.121	-.003[a]	.106	—					
7. Cable TV	.106	-.010	.166	.019	.079	.004[a]	—				
8. Newspaper	.020	.267	.140	.099	.045	-.091	.098	—			
9. Computer	-.239	-.221	.397	.312	.185	.179	.072	.025	—		
10. Internet	-.180	-.189	.348	.269	.142	.094	.098	.027	.643	—	
11. Time of survey	-.017	-.011[a]	.054	.008	.010[a]	.007[a]	.056	-.012	.091	.170	—
Mean	2.615	48.110	3.521	2.571	1.91	.78	1.750	4.632	.472	.267	16.581
s.d.	1.767	16.731	2.330	.812	.79	1.14	.433	2.701	.498	.443	10.814

Note: All correlations are statistically significant at $p < .05$, except those marked with an [a].

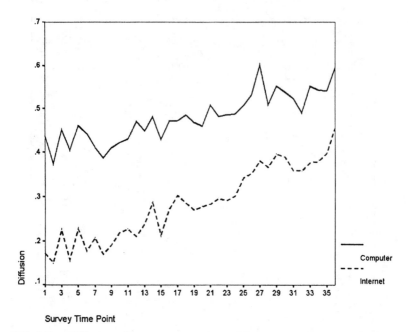

FIG. 3.2.   Diffusion of home computers and Internet access in study households.

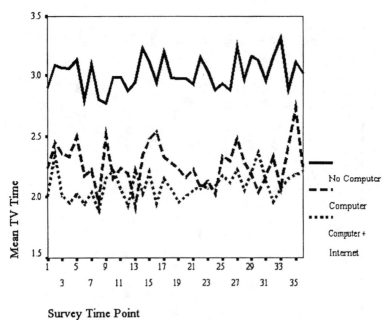

FIG. 3.3   Time spent with TV, by computer and Internet diffusion.

36

TABLE 3.2
Results of a Multiple Regression Analysis Predicting Time Spent With Television

	Beta	Block R2	Equation R2
Diffusion and Time of Survey			
Survey time point	.003[n.s.]		
November	−.034		
December	−.011[n.s.]		
February	−.021		
March	.001[n.s.]		
April	−.028		
May	−.024		
June	−.044		
July	−.020		
August	−.018		
September	−.024		
October	−.036		
		.002	.002
Demographics and Household Characteristics			
Income	−.231		
Education	−.153		
Age	.151		
Adults in household (number)	.016		
Children in household (number)	−.055		
		.137	.139
Other Media Use			
Reads newspapers (days/week)	.012		
Cable TV in home	.146		
		.021	.160

Note: Total n = 22,851. All coefficients are statistically significant at $p < .05$, except those indicated by [n.s.] (not statistically significant).

addition, diagnostic tests and examination of collinearity indicate no collinearity or singularity in the data.

All other variables are significant except for 2 months of the year. Although monthly differences in prime time have been known since the 1930s (Lumley, 1934), it is surprising to find such differences in such a gross measure as "average time" spent with television. Such a finding provides some validity to the measure of TV time used in the surveys. In addition to the seasonal (monthly) factors, education, income, age, the number of adults and children in the household, the presence of cable TV in the home, and newspaper reading are all associated with TV viewing.

The third step in the analysis was to employ a multiple regression analysis to predict the residual television viewing time by a series of variables related to the time of the study such as demographics, household characteristics, and use of other media before attempting to predict by home computer and Internet access. As is evident from Table 3.2, those factors shown to be important in previous studies are also important to our understanding of displacement effects associated with computers and the Internet. Slight seasonal variation in viewing can be seen in the significant relationships between viewing and month in which the survey took place. Various demographic and other household characteristics such as the number of adults and the number of children were also important in relation to time spent with television. Even other media, such as newspaper reading and whether or not the household had cable TV, are statistically significant predictors.

The third step in the analysis is shown in Table 3.3, which presents a conservative approach to testing Hypotheses 2 and 3. The residual TV viewing time from the analysis presented in Table 3.2 was used as the dependent variable. By using this residual we are able to examine TV viewing time after controlling for all of the factors described earlier. The first block of Table 3.3, under the heading "full sample," indicates that diffusion of both computers and the Internet are statistically significant predictors of TV time even after all the variables described previously have been controlled. There is a negative beta weight for both, indicating that higher adoption levels are associated with lower time. Thus, we find support for the first two hypotheses. There is also a significant prediction associated with the interaction of survey time point and adoption of the technologies, suggesting a possible curvilinear aspect to the data. We modeled the curvilinear aspect of the interaction by cubing the interaction variable as well, but found no significant relationship.

The third hypothesis centered on the interaction of age and computer/Internet diffusion on residual viewing time. To test the significance of the interaction between age and diffusion, we analyzed each of the subgroups separately, and these are also presented in Table 3.3. If the effect on TV time is different for the age subgroups, we should see these differences reflected in the predictive capabilities within each group. As is evident from the table, the effects within the two youngest age groups (in which all the variables are significant except for the cubed interaction term in the second age group) are considerably different from the effects within the last two age groups (where only one variable is significant in each of the groups). To help explain the data in Table 3.3, Figs. 3.4 and 3.5 depict them graphically.

The final step in the analysis was to compute an F-test for the equality of slopes for the age subgroups was conducted. For this test, the residual sum of squares within groups is compared to the regression sum of squares for all the groups (Brown, Engelman, Hill, & Jennrich, 1988). The results were statistically significant at $p < .001$. This supports Hypothesis 3 by indicating that statistically significant predictive power is added by analyzing the age groups separately, a test of the interaction of age and diffusion.

DISCUSSION AND INTERPRETATION

The analyses reported in the preceding pages support hypotheses 1 and 2, which predicted negative effects of computer and Internet adoption on time spent with television. Hypothesis 3 was partially supported. The analysis shows that age does participate in an interaction effect on TV time, but the effect is equally pronounced in the second age group (31–50) rather than, as hypothesized, among the youngest group of adults (19–30).

The interaction effects should be examined with care. Because of the use of age subgroups in Table 3.3, main effects are actually interactions (interacting with age). This means that the significant interactions of Table 3.3 are actually two-way interactions, complicating the interpretation. What is clear is that the effects are strongest for the two youngest groups (those less than 31 and those between 31 and 50). What we see here is that the interactive effects are essentially opposite to each other. Unlike most interactions in multiple regression research, the time variable provides a relatively strong base for interpretation.

In the case of those under 31, what appears to be happening is that diffusion of computers and the Internet are both associated with decreases in TV time. However, the nature of the relationship appears to be curvilinear. In terms of the first interaction, the later the computer diffused within the 3-year study period, the greater the TV time, whereas the second interaction (time by computer diffusion cubed) indicates that the later in the study the computer diffused, the less the TV time. We might interpret the first effect as one that is associated with diffusion but is not a causal process. What appears to be happening is that as computers diffuse, they reach a broader segment of the population (segments that watch more TV in general) and, thus, average time spent with TV appears to increase among those with computers. The second interaction is negative, which would be consistent with a displacement hypothesis in indicating that, after controlling for the diffusion effect described earlier, the longer a person has had a computer, the less TV he or she watches.

Among the second age group (31–50), we find an opposite effect occurring. The best interpretation would appear to be that because this group is more es-

TABLE 3.3

Analyses of residual time spent with television, diffusion of computers and the Internet and their interaction with time by the full sample and by age groups

	Beta	Block R2	Equation R2
Full Sample			
Computer diffusion	-.050		
Internet diffusion	-.042	.006	.006
Time × computer diffusion	-.056		
Time × Internet diffusion	.064		
Time × computer diffusion cubed	.012$^{n.s.}$		
Time × Internet diffusion cubed	.008$^{n.s.}$	.001	.007
For Ages < 31			
Computer diffusion	-.077		
Internet diffusion	-.052	.003	.003
Time × computer diffusion	.083		
Time × Internet diffusion	.074		
Time × computer diffusion cubed	-.113		
Time × Internet diffusion cubed	.064	.006	.009
For Ages 31–50			
Computer diffusion	-.035		

Internet diffusion	-.042	.008	.008
Time × computer diffusion	-.133		
Time × Internet diffusion	.069		
Time × computer diffusion cubed	.061		
Time × Internet diffusion cubed	.003[n.s.]	.001	.010

For Ages 51–65

Computer diffusion	-.015[n.s.]		
Internet diffusion	-.060[n.s.]	.002	.002
Time × computer diffusion	-.068[n.s.]		
Time × Internet diffusion	.076[a]		
Time × computer diffusion cubed	.036[n.s.]		
Time × Internet diffusion cubed	.015[n.s.]	.001[n.s.]	.003

For Ages 66+

Computer diffusion	-.114		
Internet diffusion	-.034[n.s.]	.004	.004
Time × computer diffusion	.113[n.s.]		
Time × Internet diffusion	.062[n.s.]		
Time × computer diffusion cubed	-.088[n.s.]		
Time × Internet diffusion cubed	-.007[n.s.]	.001[n.s.]	.006

Note: Total n = 22,851. All coefficients are statistically significant at $p < .05$, except those indicated with an [a] ($p < .10$) or [n.s.] (not statistically significant).

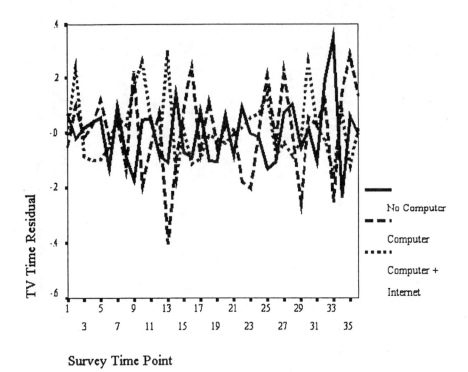

FIG. 3.4   Residual time spent with TV by computer and Internet diffusion after controlling for time of survey, demographics, household characteristics, other media use, and interaction terms.

tablished in society, income and other socioeconomic variables are less of a barrier to computer purchase than among the younger age group. The association between owning a computer and watching less television is stronger in the early part of the time series than it is later in the time period. This essentially demonstrates a displacement effect, and may be associated with the explosion in the number of websites as well as the publicity the Internet has received in the media. However, the cubed interaction suggests that for this group the displacement effect may be temporary; this is the "novelty effect" sometimes found in the media diffusion literature. If this is the case, after a certain time period in which the new medium displaces television time, there would appear to be an increase in TV viewing time. However, it is not possible to discern whether "recovery" from this novelty effect would result in this age group's watching TV at their former levels.

Although there is clearly a displacement effect, as show by the betas in Table 3.3, the depth of the displacement, as indicated by the betas and the amount of explained variance, is extremely shallow. At first glance, the findings from the Stanford study (Markoff, 2000) might be taken to indicate a

Ages 19-30

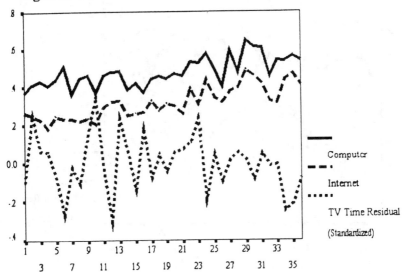

Survey Time Point

Ages 31-50

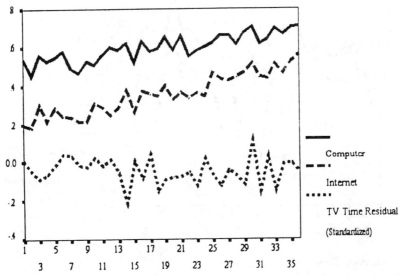

Figure 3.5 continued on next page

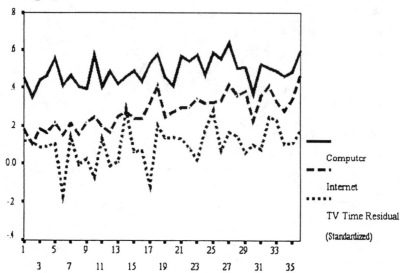

Survey Time Point

Ages 66-102

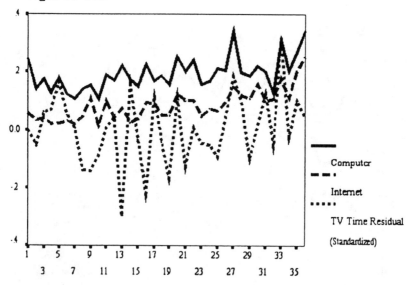

Survey Time Point

FIG. 3.5   Computer and Internet diffusion, by TV time residuals for ages 19–102.

rather deep displacement, because 59% of those online for 5 or more hours a week indicated that they had decreased their TV viewing. However, there are differences between the BSP studies used in this chapter and the Stanford study, which make comparisons quite difficult.

First, the Stanford study measured the actual magnitude of time spent with the Internet, whereas the BSP surveys asked respondents only if they had Internet access. Second, the BSP surveys measure the actual magnitude of the time spent with television, whereas the Stanford study only very roughly gauged time spent by asking respondents whether they had "increased," "decreased," or were "unchanged" in their TV viewing. These differences make it impossible to assess whether the two studies are consistent in their findings regarding displacement. It may be that self-report perceptions of changes in time spent are greater or less than the actual magnitude of changes.

In addition, it would be possible to improve the BSP measures of time spent with television. These surveys asked respondents for "average" hours and minutes of TV use, which may be difficult for the respondent to compute. The accepted practice in media studies has been to ask about time spent with media "yesterday," because the respondent can both recall and compute this information more easily than an "average." Nevertheless, the measures are sensitive enough to indicate viewing seasonality, which suggests that they are probably capturing a "real" effect. In attempting to assess the degree of displacement, future studies should measure the actual magnitude of time spent with both the Internet and TV in ways consistent with current practice in media research.

The study reported here included longitudinal data, whereas previous studies have been confined to cross-sectional studies. The cross-sectional studies asking about decreases or increases cannot provide reliable estimates of magnitude. The present study cannot rule out all other influences on the decline in television time. However, by sampling from the same population 36 times over 3 years, the present study does provide some indication of the maximum displacement effect we may expect at this point in the Internet and computer diffusion curves.

Furthermore, attention should not be confined to the Internet and television. Although television holds the largest "chunk" of time—and thus the largest opportunity for the Internet—the Internet is a diverse medium with content that is similar to that purveyed by a number of the older media. Hence, it is quite possible that displacement effects of the Internet will be manifested across several media. For example, the Stanford study respondents who used the Internet heavily had also decreased their reading of newspapers, whereas unpublished data gathered by one author of this chapter indicates that respondents who use online news sources had decreased their reading of newspapers and magazines. Although television may be a good candidate for displacement, given the amount of time accorded to the medium by viewers, it is also likely that other traditional media will suffer displacement due to the rising use and popularity of the

Internet. Other likely candidates for displacement would include the postal service and telephone.

This chapter demonstrates that displacement and other effects of new media may not be as simple and straightforward as the impression created by earlier studies would lead us to believe. Diffusion of new technologies implies adoption across age groups, but the rate of adoption is different between social strata. Time complicates our understanding of the process, because effects within social groups may be obscured by the overall diffusion rate. It is clear that further multivariate time-series designs will be required to unlock these fairly subtle effects on media and time displacement.

REFERENCES

Albarran, A. B., & Dimmick, J. (1993). An assessment of utility and competitive superiority in the video entertainment industries. *Journal of Media Economics, 6*(2), 45–52.

Anonymous. (1912) A substitute for the penny arcade. *The Outlook, 102*(26), 376–377.

Block, M. (1979). Time allocation in mass communication research. In M. Voigt & G. Hanneman (Eds.), *Progress in communication sciences* (Vol. 1; pp. 29–49). Norwood, NJ: Ablex.

Bogart, L. (1957). *The age of television.* New York: Ungar.

Brown, W., Engelman, L., Hill, M., & Jennrich, R. (1988). *BMDP statistical software manual (Volume 2).* Berkeley: University of California Press.

Cunningham & Walsh, Inc. (1958). *Videotown XI.* New York: Author.

Dimmick, J. (1993). Ecology, economics, and gratification utilities. In A. Alexander, J. Owers, & R. Carveth (Eds.), *Media economics: Theory and practice* (pp. 135–156). Hillsdale, NJ: Lawrence Erlbaum Associates.

Dimmick, J., Kline, S., & Stafford, L. (2000). The gratification niches of personal e-mail and the telephone: Competition, displacement and complementarity. *Communication Research, 27*(2), 227–248.

Dimmick, J., & Rothenbuhler, E. (1984a). The theory of the niche: Quantifying competition among mass media industries. *Journal of Communication, 34*(1), 103–119.

Dimmick, J., & Rothenbuhler, E. (1984b). Competitive displacement in the communication industries: New media in old environments. In R. Rice et al. (Eds.), *The new media* (pp. 287–304). Beverly Hills, CA: Sage.

Edwards, R. (1915). *Popular amusements.* New York: Association Press.

Find/SVP. (1997). *American user Internet survey* [online]. Available: http://etrg.findsvp.com/internet/findf.html

Graney, M. J., & Graney E. E. (1974). Communications activity substitution in aging. *Journal of Communication, 24*(4), 88–96.

Gulick, L. (1909). Popular recreation and public morality. *Annals of the Academy of Political and Social Science, 34,* 33–42.

Herzog, H. (1961). Motivations and gratifications of daily serial listeners. In W. Schramm & D. Roberts (Eds.), *The process and effects of mass communication* (pp. 50–55). Urbana: University of Illinois Press.

Hudson, T. R. (1951). *Family life habits in television and non-television homes.* Unpublished masters thesis. Stanford University, Stanford, CA.

Hurley, J. (1937). Movie and radio: Friend and foe. *The English Journal, 26*(3), 206–211.

Jones, H. (1922). Discussion—what do the people want? In *Proceedings of the National Conference of Social Work: 47th Annual* (pp. 107–109). Chicago: University of Chicago Press.

Katz, E., Gurevitch, M., & Haas, H. (1973). On the use of mass media for important things. *American Sociological Review, 38,* 164–181.

Kirkpatrick, C. (1933). *Report of a research into the attitudes and habits of radio listeners.* St. Paul, MN: Webb.

Kline, F. G. (1971). Media time budgeting as a function of demographics and lifestyle. *Journalism Quarterly, 48,* 211–221.

Kline, F. G. (1977). Time in communication research. In P. Hirsch, P. Miller, & F. G. Kline (Eds.), *Strategies for communication research* (pp. 187–204). Beverly Hills, CA: Sage.

Lumley, F. (1934). *Measurement in radio.* Columbus: Ohio State University.

Lynd, R. S., & Lynd, H. M. (1929). *Middletown.* New York: Harcourt, Brace.

Lynd, R. S., & Lynd, H. M. (1937). *Middletown revisited.* New York: Harcourt, Brace.

Markoff, J. (2000, February 16). A newer, lonelier crowd emerges in Internet study. *The New York Times,* pp. 1, 15.

Ogburn, W. F. (1933). The influence of invention and discovery. In President's Research Committee (Eds.), *Recent social trends in the United States* (Vol. 1, pp. 122–166). New York: McGraw-Hill.

Robinson, J., & Godbey, G. (1997). *Time for life* (2nd ed.). University Park: Pennsylvania State University Press.

Sorokin, P. A., & Berger, C. Q. (1939). *Time-budgets of human behavior.* Cambridge, MA: Harvard University Press.

Sterling, C. H., & Kittross, J. M. (1978). *Stay tuned.* Belmont, CA: Wadsworth.

Swanson, C., & Jones, R. (1951). Television owning and its correlates. *Journal of Applied Psychology, 35*(5), 352–357.

Sweetser, F. L. (1955). Home television and behavior: Some tentative conclusions. *Public Opinion Quarterly, 19*(1), 79–84.

Zangwill, I. (1905). The future of vaudeville in America. *The Cosmopolitan, 38,* 639–646.

4

TEMPORAL ASPECTS
OF MEDIA DISTRIBUTION [1]

Robert G. Picard
Mikko Grönlund
Turku School of Economics and Business Administration

Time is a scarce resource that is becoming increasingly significant to the media environment and media research. The temporal demands of modern society are placing increased pressure on individuals' leisure time and media use, and simultaneously placing more pressures on media and their operations.

Ironically, these temporal pressures run counter to the milieu of the god of time and watchmakers, Chronus. In Greek mythology, Cronus was a Titan who ruled the universe during the Golden Age, a period noted for its tranquillity and harmony, in which no work or other pressures interfered with contemplation and perfect happiness. But because that ideal state does not exist today, there is a good deal of concern in media circles about the time spent by consumers using media and media time use as a component of other time use (see, e.g., Becker & Schoenbach, 1989; Dewerth-Pallmeyer, 1996; Neuman, 1992; Nieto, 2000). Temporal issues

[1]For questions, contact the first author: Dr. Robert G. Picard, Media Group Business Research and Development Centre, Turku School of Economics and Business Administration, P. O. Box 110, FIN-20521, Turku, FINLAND. Phone: +358 2 3383 502; Fax: +358 2 3383 515; e-mail: Robert.Picard@tukkk.fi

also play a significant role in dictating the markets, substitutability, and operations of media.

This chapter focuses on the relations of time to the preparation for production and distribution of media products and services. In this regard, time is an economic factor that is limited by its scarcity. That temporal scarcity affects industry and company structures and costs in media industries.

In our discussion, we approach time in its linear conception, extending backward and forward, as a measurable concept. We accept that the perception of time is highly structured by social conventions, and that its import and meaning in terms of media markets and operations is affected by the dominant collective view of time in developed Western society.

We do not engage in a broader discourse of the nature of time. Thus, we lay aside the philosophical debates of Aristotle of whether time is motion, of Plato and St. Augustine that time came into existence with God's creation of the world, of Hegel and Kant that time is an illusion or a subjective part of perception, of Newton that time exists independently of events, and of Einstein that time is a means of understanding distance between events. Our use of the concept of time employs a determinist construct and how it affects the preparation and distribution of media products.

TEMPORAL ISSUES OF CONTENT PREPARATION TIME

Temporal issues regularly affect the preparation of content for distribution. The first and most evident issue is the deadline. The deadline, of course, is that hour at which content must be moved from those who write, edit, lay out, and design it to the actual processing and production for distribution.

In magazines, for example, this means the day on which content must be sent to the printers. In newspapers, it is the hour in which content must leave the newsroom so that printing activities can take place. In television news, the deadline means the point at which no changes will take place in a newscast unless an extremely important story is breaking and can be included.

The issues of deadlines are probably more crucial in newspapers than any other medium, because moving a deadline back to accommodate a major story immediately incurs monetary costs. Moving a deadline in magazines may result in delays in production and distribution, but does not immediately incur costs in most cases. Similarly, moving a deadline in news agencies is done not by postponing completion of the general news or feature bulletin, but instead adding the delayed story at a later point. A similar mechanism is used in broadcast media.

When a newspaper moves a deadline back, however, the change increases the work time of content creation, editing, and layout for personnel, and nearly always forces prepress, printing, postpress and circulation personnel to work beyond their scheduled hours. This creates additional—and often significant—wage costs. An hour's delay can easily incur thousands of dollars of costs for even a small newspaper or tens of thousands for a large one.

Another significant temporal issue involves the effects of work shifts on when content is prepared for distribution. These work shifts create production and distribution cycles for individual media units in which specific activities take place at specific times (see Picard & Brody, 1997). In domestic settings, work shifts are scheduled to meet the local demands for covering daytime events, contacting sources of news during regular office hours, and preparing content for distribution at its appointed times. International newsgathering is based on the activities that must take place at domestic bureaus or domestic media that provide coverage for news agencies, so the work shifts of those bureaus or media play a role in when information is disseminated.

Except for extraordinary coverage, magazines, newspapers, television stations, and radio stations do not fully staff their content offices 24 hours a day. Even news services rarely staff bureaus throughout the day and only partly staff regional news distribution centers on a full-day basis.

As a result, news that occurs overnight in Santiago, Chile, may not be prepared by a news bureau there and forwarded to a regional news center in Buenos Aires until the morning of the following day, unless it is a very large story warranting overtime efforts by the staff. Similarly, that news may be forwarded to media in Tokyo, Japan, but not prepared for broadcast or printing until the next day, because it may arrive between deadlines due to time zone differences.

ISSUES OF PHYSICAL DISTRIBUTION TIME

Significant temporal factors affect the time required for media content to be transferred to users. Print media face significant temporal issues in distribution, because physical products are involved and the issues are especially strong for newspaper and magazines. These issues also affect physical audio and visual materials such as CDs, videos, and DVDs, but to a lesser degree than they do media providing contemporary information.

Daily newspapers, for example, require same-day distribution if content is to be current and competitive with other daily information sources. In terms of distribution, this means that newspapers must be delivered in a timely manner to kiosks, newsstands, and other distribution points so that they are available to consumers at the expected morning or afternoon period.

In many locations, reading and lifestyle habits require home delivery of subscribed newspapers. The simplest and easiest method that can be employed for this purpose is the use of the post. If local custom requires morning delivery, postal distribution can be problematic because few postal systems are able to guarantee delivery prior to commuting or working hours. In many nations, including developed nations in Europe and North America, the postal systems are unable to guarantee even same-day, much less early morning, distribution locally or nationally.

This presents a significant problem for newspaper firms, because the news content is typically 12 to 24 hours old when the paper is printed. If the post cannot deliver the paper until the day after publication, the paper is put into the position of providing yesterday's news tomorrow. This is clearly a competitive disadvantage by comparison to broadcast, online, and other news sources.

As a result, this temporal problem forces newspapers that want to have home delivery to establish their own home distribution systems, individually or jointly with other newspapers. But even with such a distribution mechanism, temporal constraints limit the distances at which papers can be delivered in a timely manner. This factor—along with reader demands for local content and advertiser demand for local audiences—is why newspapers tend to serve rather compact local geographic markets, and can serve national markets only in small nations unless satellite printing facilities are used.

In Finland, for example, newspaper delivery is expected at subscribers' homes in urban areas prior to 6:00 A.M. to allow subscribers time to read prior to their morning departure. Readers, as well as advertisers who want to promote sales and events on the same day that the paper is distributed, demand this delivery time. If the newspaper arrives too late for reading before subscribers leave their homes or after subscribers have departed, the news becomes stale and the advertising is rendered ineffective. To meet the time constraint, Finnish newspapers use a combination of special postal delivery and self-distribution systems.

The time constraints on newspapers are amplified when cross-border distribution is involved, because customs inspection time as well as the additional time for transfer between national postal and other distribution systems is required.

There is, however, a small international trade in newspapers that primarily serves travelers, government officials, and businesses needing significant and regular information about another country, as well as libraries and researchers. Because of the type of use these consumers make of the newspapers, the temporal factor is less important and they are sometimes willing to accept delays of a few days or even a week in distribution. Even within Europe, where internal trade and customs systems have been simplified by the common market, international newspaper trade is limited and amounts to only about 1% of the total newspaper circulation (Office of Official Publications of the European Union, 2000).

Magazines face similar time constraints in distribution but the pressure is somewhat lessened, especially for monthly magazines. Weekly publications, whether public affairs magazines or general magazines, face the same problems as newspapers in that their content is typically tied to contemporary events and their coverage must be deemed by readers as current.

In most nations, distribution to kiosks and newsstands can be accomplished within 24 to 48 hours because a variety of types of distribution systems operated by commercial or cooperative firms exist to serve this purpose. Similarly, domestic postal systems are typically able to deliver magazines to home or business subscribers within 48 to 72 hours.

Internationally, however, distribution of magazines can take between 1 to 3 weeks among developed nations unless specialized distribution services are employed or reciprocal contracts among domestic magazine distribution systems speed the process. For single-copy sales, both the costs of such specialized distribution services and the number of unsold copies are high, making the situation undesirable. In total, only about 4% of the circulation of magazines in the European Union (EU) crosses any national border (*Cross Border Distribution and Pricing,* 1997). As a result of temporal and cost issues, as well as linguistic issues, the magazine industry structure tends to be national and dominated by domestic titles.

The physical distribution of books faces far fewer temporal constraints than that of newspapers and magazines, because their content is not so dated by immediacy requirements. They are not without their own temporal requirements for books on current affairs or strong unexpected demand for specific titles; but these requirements can typically be met by traditional and rapid cargo delivery services.

In the global setting, however, distribution between continents is often problematic and can add months to distribution time. In order to overcome some of the global temporal problems of book distribution and marketing, many publishers sell regional, as well as linguistic, rights to their titles, so that the problems of general distribution from North America to Europe or Europe to Asia are avoided.

Note, though, that the problem of book distribution has become significant for firms engaged in electronic commerce of books. Consumers who select and purchase books online tend to expect fairly immediate fulfillment of their purchases. This problem is compounded because most online booksellers stock only a limited number of titles themselves and rely on publishers' distribution systems to ship orders that are passed on by the online firms. Although many publishing companies attempt to process orders within 2 to 3 days, some firms take weeks, and this can create unhappy relations among the customer, bookseller, and publisher.

Even when an order is filled, the parcel must be dispatched to customers through a commercial or postal distribution system, a process that can take between 48 hours and 3 weeks depending on the method and price of distribution selected. When transborder shipment is involved, the distribution process can add 2 days to 2 weeks to the time requirements, depending on the efficiency of customs services.

In most ways, the physical distribution times for audio and video recordings are affected by temporal problems similar to those encountered by books. But international regional distribution practices and piracy issues resulting from the nature of these products also affect audio and video temporal distribution issues.

Audio and video products created in the United States, for example, are typically released later in Europe, Latin America, Asia, and Africa. This occurs because of distribution requirements for physical copies, requirements for secure transportation of master tapes or copies from which copies for those regions will be produced, and the subtitling or dubbing of video products. The temporal delays create problems for both industries.

Recordings of popular artists made available for sale in the United States and Europe prior to their release elsewhere are often transformed into digital files that are available on the Internet and violate the copyrights of the songwriters, publishers, artists, and recording companies. These digital files can lower demand for the recordings once they are officially released. Sometimes these Internet files include not merely single songs but all the songs on a CD. These files can be used to create counterfeit recordings for sale in regions where they are not yet available in stores, as well as cheaper recordings than the authorized versions available in shops.

The delays also promote pirated copies of motion pictures that are achieving success in the United States and elsewhere. These regularly appear in video or DVD form worldwide before their global theatrical release. Sometimes pirated video recordings of popularly anticipated films appear even before their initial release, because of the time between final edit and transportation of copies to theaters.

The temporal problems creating these delays are being addressed by major media firms and are an impetus toward greater globalization by major media firms.

THE PRICE OF PHYSICAL DISTRIBUTION TIME

As noted earlier, there is a link between distribution time and cost for media with physical form. This economic factor in distribution involves both costs for distribution services and the fact that providing distribution in less time is more expensive. As illustrated in Fig. 4.1, when the time available between completion of production and delivery is short, distribution costs are highest, but they decline as the time available increases. This occurs because when it is possible to take more time, the materials can be combined with others materials being shipped, to gain savings by efficient use of truck, rail, aircraft, ships, and other transportation methods.

A German book publisher who needs to deliver 20 boxes of books to a bookshop in London by 9:00 A.M. tomorrow morning illustrates this problem. To ensure on-time delivery, the publisher will need to use either an express delivery service or its own delivery personnel and truck to send the shipment by ferry. However, if the books are not needed for 5 days, a traditional freight delivery service can be used at great cost savings.

ISSUES IN DISTRIBUTION TIME OF NONPHYSICAL MEDIA

The actual distribution of physical products is not a problem for nonphysical media based on analog and digital signals. Nevertheless, such media encounter a variety of temporal issues.

In broadcast media such as radio and television, for example, the broadcast distribution and reception of material by audiences is simultaneous, so broadcasters create and distribute material intended for certain audiences

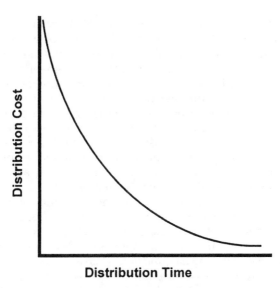

Distribution Time

FIG. 4.1   Effect of distribution time on distribution cost.

available at different times of the day. The possibility of targeting materials to those available in various dayparts allows broadcasters to seek audiences who are preparing to go or are already traveling to work in the morning, those who are at home or in their workplaces during the day, those who are traveling home in the evening, and the more general audience at home in the evening.

A certain amount of time shifting is possible if consumers use recording devices such as videocassette recorders, but temporal constraints essentially mean that most audiences receive materials when they are broadcast. Even when VCRs are used for time shifting, advertisers are wary of the value of the audience. This limitation has led to efforts by the broadcasting industry to find ways to create digital television on demand that will increase the ability and ease with which audiences can accomplish time shifting of reception. Thus, audiences can be more effectively measured for advertisers.

Broadcasting is also affected by time zones. A major sporting event, such as the Formula 1 race at Suzuki, Japan, will be run and broadcast in the daytime in Japan, but the live broadcast will be received in the very early morning in Europe. These types of temporal issues are usually overcome by rebroadcasting later in the day or using a tape delay in which video of the event is received live by broadcasters but not distributed to their viewers until later.

The problems of time zones are problematic for media in nations that are geographically large on the East–West axis, cross more than one meridian of longitude, and have multiple time zones. In the United States, for example, when it is 7:00 P.M. in Washington, D.C., it is 4:00 P.M. in Los Angeles and 3:00

P.M. in parts of Alaska. Russia suffers similar problems in reverse. When it is 7:00 P.M. in Moscow, it is 2:00 A.M. the following morning in Vladivostok.

These problems make it difficult to broadcast news and entertainment nationally without use of local tape delays. Although tape delays are not a particularly significant disadvantage when entertainment programming is involved, they date the information involved in news programming. When the national evening news is broadcast in the United States, for example, it is broadcast live for the Eastern and Central portions of the country but then rebroadcast for the West Coast, Alaska, and Hawaii. In order to make the news more current, the news hosts make the initial live broadcast, have dinner, and then return to broadcast both updated stories as well as tape-delayed portions of the original broadcast.

For global broadcast media, the differences in time zones present even more difficult operational problems when news and other time-sensitive information is involved. If the broadcast firm is large enough, such as CNN, it has the opportunity for 24-hour news operations. Even then, because most news is created during daytime hours across time zones, global operations with a fixed broadcast base create work-shift and production cycle problems at the site of the global broadcast and separate the base from the daytime region in which news is occurring.

One answer to this issue is the creation of regional broadcast centers in three locations, each corresponding to a group of 8-hour time periods. These might be, for example, located in New York, London, and Tokyo. As the workday ends in one location, the primary broadcasting can be passed off to the next location. This process, borrowed for multinational corporations and some superpower government agencies, permits global 24-hour operations with primary staffing only during normal working hours but allows the full range of company services to be offered simultaneously everywhere in the world. This pattern of operation is increasingly being integrated into Cable News Network (CNN) and may appear more strongly in BBC World, Sky News, Deutche Welle, NHK, and other operations attempting to provide global, round-the-clock news operations.

News agencies such as Reuters, Associated Press, and Agence France Presse have not yet adopted the revolving global operations model, although they distribute analog and digital nonphysical products. This is because the structure of agencies is based on domestic news operations that feed regional news operations, and ultimately service global operations. As a result, the primary sources of news and information preparation and distribution are the domestic and regional news centers rather than a global center that produces material for the regions and nations. As noted previously, this structure creates some delays in global distribution unless the news is a highly significant story that merits a special bulletin.

The Internet also presents temporal issues for major content providers. It has some of the immediacy of live broadcasting, but the age of its news and contemporary information typically falls somewhere between that of broadcasting and newspapers. This occurs for three reasons.

First, the time of distribution and time of reception are not simultaneous for most Internet material providers and audiences. Even active users of the Internet check for material primarily in the morning or evening, and sometimes during the day if they have computers with Internet access at their workplace. This means they go for hours at a time without attending to contemporary news or information that may be distributed by Internet content services. The hours of use issue is compounded by the physical connection required for use. Electronic manufacturers, however, are developing wireless applications to allow for mobile connectivity that can be used by individuals to acquire information when they are away from their computers.

Second, news and other contemporary information available on the Internet, with the exception of real-time financial data, are distributed by news services that gather and distribute information in a manner similar to their distribution of scheduled news bulletins to other media. As a result, news available by the Internet becomes dependent on the work shifts and work flows of media, so information may have been distributed as much as 24 hours prior to the report's Internet publication, depending on the news service. Admittedly, the majority of major news providers for Internet portals—such as the world's top news agencies—update material more frequently, but it is not unusual for the news to have been originally distributed 2 to 8 hours before.

Third, both commercial and institutional Internet service providers have been struggling with issues of service interruptions and reliability. Although the major service providers tend to have the best systems and servers, and often have backup systems that are used in the event of problems, service disruptions have not been uncommon in recent years. These typically delay the arrival of content material. Institutional service providers, such as universities and companies offering access through their networks, are not hampered by customer service demands of commercial service providers and tend to have fewer backup systems. As a result, it is not unusual for those who rely on such institutional service providers to find servers down for maintenance or other problems for significant periods of time.

Because of its global nature and the manner in which it spans time zones, the Internet presents temporal problems with regard to scheduling online meetings and events, downloading material, and other Internet-based applications. To help overcome this problem, an alternative time measurement, Internet Time, has been introduced. Internet Time is not based on time zones, and is not affected by daylight savings time changes. Instead, it divides the day into 1,000 beat counts. Although not quite the "star date" of *Star Trek* notoriety, Internet Time provides a workable means of overcoming some of the global temporal problems (http://www.swatch.com/internettime/).

TEMPORAL ISSUES IN MARKETING

The time required to market media products and services is related to the relations of media with consumers and the frequency of their publication or release. Marketing and promotional efforts for motion pictures, for example, begin prior to the beginning of production, continue during filming, and increase in intensity during postproduction and release periods. Thus, the marketing of motion pictures is often a 2-year activity. This lengthy lead time for marketing is required because each film is an individual product and the audience for each film differs from that of previous films.

Similarly, the marketing time for TV programs ranges from 3 months to 2 years prior to broadcast, depending on the nature of the program. For programs resulting from acceptances of initial concept pitches to broadcasters, marketing the program to consumers will begin concurrently with the production of initial episodes. For a large-scale costume drama, miniseries, or similar production, marketing will also begin with production, often as much as 1 year prior to broadcast. Syndicated off-network programs will be made available to other broadcasters 1 to 2 years prior to broadcast, and consumer marketing may also begin 3 to 6 months prior to broadcast. As with films, television programs are individual products and need individual marketing. This requirement combines with the lead time for production and broadcast scheduling to result in long marketing periods for the products.

Books, audio products, and video media also offer individual products to consumers. These media require separate marketing efforts that typically begin 2 to 3 months prior to release, and continue if the release enjoys prolonged success.

Two types of print media do not enjoy significant lead time for marketing: newspapers and magazines. Because of the frequency of their appearance and the need to keep content contemporary, it is difficult for either to engage in significant marketing of the content of individual editions. The primary means for counteracting this problem is subscribed circulation.

By marketing subscriptions, these print media reduce the specific content choices of audiences and instead sell a branded consistency of type and quality of content. Most marketing efforts in such media go toward establishing and nurturing the brand image, subscription sales, and single-copy sales based on the brand rather than specific content. These activities help overcome the temporal problems of marketing media products that are frequently available.

Only a small amount of marketing effort goes to promotion of specific content, such as posters of the day's most intriguing headlines that are delivered to news agents along with newspaper copies, or posters of a magazine's cover that are delivered to kiosks and other sites that sell single copies of magazines.

CONCLUSIONS

Although a number of temporal issues affect the market structure and operations of media, the primary contributor is the time sensitivity of the medium or, more specifically, the content that it conveys. Media industries vary greatly in terms of time sensitivity, reflecting the different roles they play for audiences. Differences in their relative sensitivity are shown in Fig. 4.2. These differences in sensitivity affect the locations from which audiences can be served, the production and distribution operations of media, and the substitutability of media.

The lessened substitutability of media is an important contributor to the structure of units of both a medium and media overall. Audiences desiring information with immediacy are not well served by news magazines, books, or informational CDs. Individuals wanting contemporary information through news magazines are not well served by news magazines from other nations or regions because of the distribution time involved. Likewise, individuals needing a daily newspaper before 7 A.M. would probably not find newspapers from distant localities useful.

Temporal issues, then, are significant economic factors that affect the structures, competition, and marketing efforts of media firms. An understanding of their impact is needed to better comprehend the intricacies of media economics and the effects they have on the availability of content.

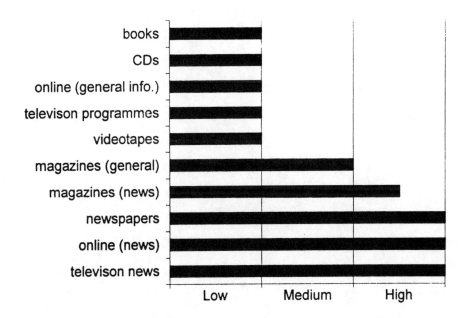

FIG. 4.2   Time sensitivity of selected media.

REFERENCES

Becker, L., & Schoenbach, K. (1989). *Audience responses to media diversification: Coping with plenty.* Mahwah, NJ: Lawrence Erlbaum Associates.
Cross border distribution and pricing. (1997). Unpublished report by NOP Research Group and Euro Strategy Consultants for European Commission, Directorate General XV (Internal Market and Financial Services).
Dewerth-Pallmeyer, D. (1996). *The audience in the news.* Mahwah, NJ: Lawrence Erlbaum Associates.
Neuman, W. R. (1992). *The future of the mass audience.* Cambridge, UK: Cambridge University Press.
Nieto, A. (2000). *Time and the information market.* Pamplona: EUNSA.
Office of Official Publications of the European Union. (2000). *Competitiveness of the European Union publishing industries.* Luxembourg: Author.
Picard, R. G., & Brody, J. H. (1997). *The newspaper publishing industry.* Boston: Allyn & Bacon.

5

THE IMPACT OF CONCENTRATION AND CONVERGENCE ON MANAGERIAL EFFICIENCIES OF TIME AND COST

Dan Shaver
Mary Alice Shaver
Michigan State University

Media organizations enter the 21st century amid unprecedented levels of change. Companies are scrambling to redefine themselves as content providers instead of newspapers, television stations, magazine publishers, or holders of other traditional media franchises. Media concentration, long a factor in print media, is accelerating at a breakneck pace across all media segments as a result of economic, technological, and regulatory changes.

Traditional media structures are undergoing rapid and dramatic alteration in many dimensions. The growth of global trade and capital markets provides the economic resources and incentives for multinational corporations to develop international media empires. At the same time, global communications technologies provide the capability for coordination and management of diverse media outlets from centralized locations. CNN, for example, can package and deliver carefully tailored and timely programming to highly segmented global markets via satellite from its Atlanta, Georgia, headquarters.

Concentration, long a factor in providing efficiencies of time in both information gathering and delivery, is a significant force driving these evolving media structures. Conglomerates, anxious to leverage content across delivery platforms that are both converging and multiplying, are diversifying their media holdings to create vertically integrated content generation and delivery chains designed to increase both efficiency and profitability.

The role of convergence in this shifting media landscape is more ambiguous because, despite its common usage in both academic and professional discourse, a clear, generally accepted definition has not yet evolved. This discussion distinguishes between two types of convergence—technological and economic.

Technological convergence is defined as the process in which distribution channels are reduced whereas content broadens. The evolution of digital delivery systems illustrates technological convergence. Online news products that incorporate traditional print elements (words and still photography) with traditional broadcast elements (motion and sound) and deliver both through a single delivery channel (a computer connected to the Internet) are an everyday example. Technological convergence is heavily dependent on the existence of an appropriate infrastructure. For the World Wide Web, for example, that means available bandwidth; hardware and software that can support sound, video streaming, and other relevant capabilities; and an audience equipped with both the knowledge and resources to access the information.

Economic convergence describes the evolution of traditional media firms to embrace activities in multiple media formats. Historically, media companies have tended to be organized along industry lines. Newspaper companies tended to publish newspapers with, perhaps, related interests in other economic activities related to the vertical economics of their industry, such as newsprint production or transportation. Even when such companies owned assets in more than one medium (e.g., broadcast properties as well as newspapers), the separate industrial segments tended to be operated as independent entities with little or no efforts to share content or resources. In part, this separation was due to regulations limiting cross-ownership in individual markets, but there also existed little economic incentive or technological support for sharing of content and audiences.

Economic convergence is the combined result of enhanced marketing opportunities provided by technological convergence and the recognition of economic advantage and efficiencies to be gained by leveraging content generated for distribution through one channel into products suitable for delivery through other media channels. This can be achieved through direct repackaging of content (as CNN achieves with much of its news content) or through product extensions (as when a newspaper company repackages its sports coverage of a championship sports team into book format for sale to fans).

To understand the impact of these changes on media behavior requires applying economic theory and traditional research to these evolving relationships. This study focuses on the implications of concentration and convergence for media companies with regard to time efficiencies. The study examines trends over the period 1994 through 1999 by looking at industry data from major U.S. media organizations. Although these companies are headquartered in the United States, many of them are global in scope.

The set of variables affecting concentration and convergence trends and their relationship to the pursuit of time and cost efficiencies is complex, and many of these variables exceed the scope of the present analysis. To explore the key relationships, we begin with a model that identifies the primary variables and then explore the implications of data drawn from eight companies for the relationship among efficiencies, convergence, and concentration among media organizations. The model is presented in Fig. 5.1.

INDUSTRY CONTEXT

Economic theory shows that market concentration offers increased possibilities for managerial economies through consolidation of management functions, increased purchasing power, reduced sales and distribution costs, and improved access to capital. Increased control over advertising pricing may result in additional revenue with little or no additional time spent generating it. In addition, increased concentration may be highly correlated with product price inelasticity (for consumers and advertisers) and a decrease in desirable substitution options for consumers.

Newspaper concentration trends have been well documented. More than a decade ago, Picard (1988) found that the eight largest newspaper groups controlled 23.5% of total newspaper circulation. The study also re-

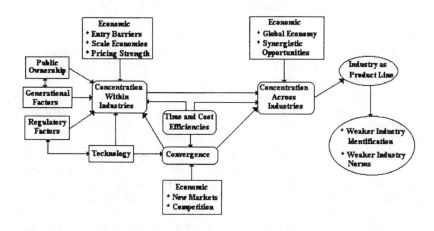

FIG. 5.1   A model of primary variables affecting concentration and convergence trends.

vealed economic concentration rates for the top 100 markets to be more than 80% and noted that economists consider rates above 50% to represent highly concentrated industries with the potential for monopolistic power. The trend has not abated in the last decade. A number of factors can be cited as contributing.

Economic barriers to entering the daily newspaper market mean that initiatives to create a new daily publication are rare, whereas failure rates for newspapers in competitive markets are high. The generation effect and economic disadvantages of scale are creating steadily mounting pressures on family newspapers to sell to chains. The generation effect means that the longer newspaper ownership remains within a family, the more splintered the ownership becomes and the larger the percentage of ownership held by family members who have no direct interest—other than simple economics—in newspaper publishing. At some point, the economic demands of nonparticipant shareholders or tax codes mount to a level where the sale of the newspaper is virtually forced. The disadvantages of scale refer to the inability of family-owned newspapers to negotiate favorable pricing for specialized capital equipment such as presses and newsroom systems. Vendors dealing with a group are likely to offer discounted pricing and superior service in hope of selling multiple systems. Those incentives don't exist with smaller operations. Disadvantages of scale exist in other areas as well—from the negotiation of long-term newsprint contracts at favorable rates to the purchase of delivery fleets.

As competitors, chain owners appear to have another advantage over local owners—greater pricing strength. Busterna (1991) found that a newspaper chain is able to charge higher rates for national advertising than is a matched set of independent newspapers.

The growing concentration of newspapers under group ownership fuels another dynamic—public ownership and a heightened emphasis on profitability. The number of newspaper groups that have turned to public ownership as a solution to the problem of generating capital for expansion and improvements has steadily increased since the early 1970s. In a 1994 study of 17 publicly traded newspaper companies, Picard (1994) found that institutional investors owned shares in all the companies studied. Picard's analysis revealed that levels of institutional ownership in almost one third of the companies studied was great enough to raise questions about potential influence over company strategy and operations.

A study by Lacy, Shaver, and St. Cyr (1996) suggested that the influence of investors may have at least indirect impact on nonfinancial performance. The authors concluded that high levels of stock ownership outside the media group resulted in increased shareholder returns and that the effect was only moderated by the impact of competitive markets. A study of newspaper publishers (Matthews, 1996) found that publishers of privately held newspapers had greater autonomy over issues of staffing and content change than did publishers in publicly held groups, and that publishers of privately held newspapers reported less pressure to generate revenue.

The trend toward concentration in the broadcast industries appears to be even sharper when regulatory restrictions are removed. The Telecommunications Act of 1996 removed most restrictions on radio ownership and ignited a wildfire of acquisitions. In an address to the National Association of Broadcasters in October 1996, FCC Commissioner Susan Ness reported a 75% increase in station transfer applications in the first 9 months after deregulation over the same period in the year before deregulation. This number, she said, affected one out of every three stations in the country (Taylor, 1996). *Broadcasting & Cable Magazine,* a trade publication, cited industry sources as saying that the cash-flow multiples paid for radio stations in 1997 were the highest in history, with ratios ranging from 13 to 18 times cash flow in large markets to 8 to 10 times cash flow in small markets (Brown, 1998).

The same story quoted Peter Handy of Star Media Group as saying that radio consolidation in the top 75 markets was 80% complete, whereas in markets 76 through 200 some 50% to 60% of stations were available for consolidation. Handy also noted that larger groups absorbed 4 of the top 25 radio groups during 1997. The report cited other industry watchers as predicting an accelerated focus on consolidation in smaller markets, noting that the top 10 radio groups owned more than 1,200 stations (primarily in top markets), but that there were still 7,500 other commercial stations in smaller markets.

The effects of this consolidation had a dramatic impact on both radio operations and audiences. Anxious to reduce costs, groups with large investments in new stations began replacing local programming with syndicated content that has proven audience appeal (Rathbun, 1996). Another common cost-reduction technique is to eliminate jobs by clustering stations in a market, replacing individual station managers with group managers, and then consolidating administrative, marketing, and engineering functions. The Radio CFO Group, sponsored by the Broadcast Cable Financial Management Association, reported in 1996 that their membership declined by 20% because of layoffs or fears of being laid off (McClellan, 1996).

Lawrence Grossman (1998), former president of NBC News and PBS, charged that cost-cutters have slashed costs and resources for news coverage while using smoke and mirrors to fool the audience. Grossman cited as evidence:

- Out of approximately 10,000 commercial radio stations throughout the nation, only about 15 are all-news outlets that employ a substantial news staff to report on their communities. All but two of those were owned by CBS.
- With deregulation, radio stations are no longer required to broadcast news or public affairs, and many don't.
- The medium has become dominated by talk shows, celebrity disc jockeys, and syndicated headline services, thus driving the disappearance of serious news reporting. Lower production costs and higher revenues are part of the entertainment-only format's success.

- Group owners have slashed station budgets and eliminated what they view as costly nonessential operating expenses such as news staffs and wire services. Instead, they have been "outsourcing" the news function to headline news services without letting their audiences know. These services use a single announcer to serve as many as 8 to 10 stations in a market, employing few if any reporters and often cannibalizing local newspapers and cable news channels for content. However, they are cheap—instead of charging station owners a fee, they provide their services in exchange for a 10-second spot after each newscast, which they resell.
- A growing number of stations are brokering their program schedules, selling blocks of time to entrepreneurs for infomercials disguised as news. For $250 per 2½-minute segment, you can actually buy an interview on one of Washington, D.C.'s three business news stations. For $1,500, you can buy an hour. This blurs the line between editorial content and advertising.

Grossman's rather glum analysis echoes findings of a study conducted after the deregulation process began lifting content requirements but before the easing of ownership restrictions led to massive concentration of ownership. McKean and Stone (1992) concluded that there was evidence that news operations were dropped for economic reasons after, and perhaps as a result of, deregulation.

Concentration of ownership in the broadcast television industry is occurring but at a slower pace than in radio, primarily because of continued ownership regulation. Economic concentration, on the other hand, appears to have been significantly limited by cable growth, satellite signal delivery and the growth of numbers of stations. Powers (1990) concluded that the advent of cable and low-power television stations had increased levels of competition and altered the market structure from that of an oligopoly to that of monopolistic competition. Bates (1993) revisited the question and reached the same conclusions regarding changes in market structure. Bates noted that concentration in television markets declined over time.

Ownership consolidation is also having an impact on the cable industry. One study identified a trend toward concentration of ownership through mergers between large multiple-system operators that began in 1985 and accelerated after 1993 (Chan-Olmsted, 1996). Largely deregulated by the Cable Communications Policy Act of 1984, the cable industry grew dramatically but failed to develop the levels of innovation and competition that the legislation was intended to foster. Spurred by complaints about undue market power adversely affecting consumers, programmers, and competing video distribution companies, the 1992 act directed the FCC to set limits on cable market concentration. Although the industry remains only moderately concentrated, it has attained the highest degree of concentration in 20 years because of horizontal mergers aimed at creating efficient market clusters.

Chan-Olmstead additionally maintained that deregulation of the telephone industry also became a factor with the 1991 U.S. District Court ruling that cleared the way for telephone companies to provide a wide range of information services and delivery of third-party video. Then, a 1995 federal court ruling in a suit brought by the U.S. Telephone Association cleared the way for almost all the regional Bell operating companies to enter the cable market. This set the stage for either competition or alliances between the two competing factions.

Newer and less-well-documented trends toward concentration appear to be developing in two other media industries. Outdoor advertising shows signs of consolidation. In 1997, Outdoor Systems, the country's largest billboard company, announced plans to acquire 3M's National Advertising Co., the U.S.'s No. 3 outdoor concern. This represented the company's 12th acquisition in a year and gave Outdoor Systems a major presence in 20 of the country's top 25 markets and control of 15% to 18% of the industry. Industry analysts predicted higher rates in cities where Outdoor Systems has a major presence. They also predicted that outdoor advertising revenues would grow from 2.2% of total ad spending to 3% within 5 years, as a result of less industry fragmentation (Brodesser, 1997).

Although relatively undocumented, the Internet is showing signs of increasing both concentration in key consumer areas and public ownership. The pattern of acquisitions by AOL of competing hosting services and of Netscape is one indicator of consolidation. Another is the increasing presence, individually and through alliances with other media companies, of newspaper and broadcast groups. With deep pockets and a firm commitment to defending and expanding their franchises, it is reasonable to suppose that they will bring the same priorities regarding profitability and news resource allocations to the Web that they apply to their traditional products. Of course, AOL has now merged with Time Warner to create new markets for Time Warner content.

But industry level consolidation is only a part of the story. Concentration and consolidation are occurring across industries as transnational media corporations gobble up newspapers, movie companies, broadcast groups, and networks. Gershon (1993) identified the driving forces behind the growth of transnational media conglomerates as an increasing emphasis on deregulation and free market economies coupled with the opportunities to develop competitive advantage and corporate strategies emphasizing vertical integration.

McChesney (1999) argued that development of primarily North American-based transnational media conglomerates since the 1980s resulted in the domination of world communications by fewer than 50 firms. This group of firms consists of a first tier of nine firms with 1997 annual revenues ranging from $6 billion to $24 billion, and a second tier of three dozen to four dozen firms whose annual revenues ranged from $1 to $8 billion. These firms are characterized by rapid growth; diversified media holdings in areas ranging from film, book publishing, television channels, amusement parks, and retail stores to newspapers; and synergistic business strategies that allow them to leverage commercial opportunities among their business lines. For example, a film may also generate a soundtrack, a book, related merchandising opportunities, possible television spin-offs, CD-ROMs, video games, and amusement park rides.

Below the major players in the media conglomerate food chain, McChesney (1999) identified several dozen smaller players that fill regional or niche markets with revenues in the range of $1 to $9 billion. The author predicted that a few of these companies would attempt aggressive growth and become first-tier global media firms.

This cross-industry consolidation has several implications for the direction of media. First, it undermines the concept of industry. An industry is generally considered to consist of a set of businesses offering generally comparable products or services to approximately the same market or kind of market of customers. A newspaper may not have direct daily newspaper competition in its primary market but still—because of similarities of product, operations, economics, and customer base—remains a part of the newspaper industry and shares many common problems and concerns with daily newspapers published across the country. The industry concept, among other things, creates an identity, allows for the formation of industry organizations like NAA to act as a voice for common issues, and facilitates government measures and comparisons of economic activity. Workers tend to identify themselves professionally with the industry and its professional norms and standards.

Inclusion in a media conglomerate, particularly one with a strategic plan that emphasizes the leveraging of content and capabilities across media platforms, tends to shift workers' sense of perspective and identity, weakening attachment to the old industry and strengthening identification with the employer. In this process, identification with industry-based norms and standards weakens and the influence of the corporate culture is strengthened. The focus of questioning shifts from "How does this compare to my industry's standards?" to "How can this be done to maximize transferability?"

The second major implication for the direction of media—a shift in conceptualization of the nature of the business—is related to the weakening of industry identification. As media companies are incorporated into transnational conglomerates, their new owners are less likely to consider them from an industrial perspective and are more likely to consider them as product lines. The key issue here involves ownership perspective rather than worker perspective. Owners control the flow of capital required for maintenance and expansion to the enterprise and exercise considerable influence, if not total control, over policies and goals. Decisions in these areas made by owners *within* an industry are more likely to be shaped by the traditional norms, industry-specific competitive considerations, and traditional social values of the industry than are owners of a media conglomerate faced with allocating limited funds among a variety of product lines with competing needs and traditions. Media conglomerate management, seeking the greatest return for its investment, is more likely to shape funding in ways that enhance synergistic returns by strengthening interaction among media product lines than to strengthen traditional industry functions. This, in turn, deepens the gulf between the individual firm/practitioner and its industry.

Convergence brings efficiencies in time spent on multiple delivery systems and purchasing power, but the amount of efficiency gained varies by media due to differences in time that must be spent on information gathering and processing. Opportunities for gains in managerial efficiencies are created as the product generated by one component of the company is channeled through the initial component into multiple yet differing types of delivery systems. These gains may be modified, however, by increased costs related to employees and added processes as the functions expand. Time efficiency, therefore, varies according to the types of media involved.

It is difficult to unhook convergence from the streams of concentration, because they are closely connected. Obviously, technological capabilities are a necessary prerequisite for convergence, but the purpose of this study is not to analyze technology in detail, but rather to investigate the implications for time and management efficiency. In its broadest form, convergence might be considered to have begun when wire services like the Associated Press began to provide news materials gathered by print journalists to electronic journalists for use in radio and television broadcasts. That represents the kernel of the central theme behind media convergence— media workers generate information content and the delivery system becomes important only as a delivery channel to specific audiences. The public statement of this sentiment began in the 1970s as media companies, particularly newspaper firms, began to perceive the opportunities and threats to their existing franchise inherent in the development of new forms of electronic delivery and new audience formation. Early endeavors like the Knight-Ridder/AT&T Viewtron experiment were unsuccessful as commercial enterprises but were successful in broadening the vision of corporate management beyond their traditional print-focused perspective. Companies began to change their names to cut the links to their industry-specific origins and to emphasize their new mission of information/content development and packaging. For example, Knight-Ridder Newspapers became Knight-Ridder; Gannett Newspapers became simply Gannett.

Various newspaper groups have experimented with a number of ways to leverage their core competencies in content generation into new delivery systems and markets. Development of local cable news programming; evolving in-house photography capability into commercial services; electronic delivery of specialized business and market information; and electronic database publishing, magazine publishing, and book publishing have all been attempted by one group or another with various degrees of success.

The exponential growth of the World Wide Web, however, provided an irresistible opportunity. Early Internet adopters represented a small but (from the perspective of marketing demographics) intensely desirable audience. And although the Internet audience was small, even into the mid-1990s, its growth curve was exponential. A study of primary news sources found the overwhelming majority of online consumers of news were younger college graduates with incomes in excess of $40,000 (Stempel & Hargrove, 1996). This, coupled with the perception that specialized online services offering databases for used cars, job opportunities, and real estate listings represented a significant threat to the major classified revenue streams that comprise approximately 40% of the average daily newspaper's advertising income, compelled publishers to feel that they had to establish an online presence.

The rush of newspapers to the web is well documented. Middleberg and Ross (1997) found that 55% of newspapers were already online and that only 9% indicated they had no current plans to establish online editions.

Griswold (1998) noted that newspapers' initial reasons for going online tended to be more strategic than profit oriented. The author reported that 56% of respondents indicated that their initial reasons were "defensive"; whereas 22% indicated a desire simply to establish an online presence, and 22% cited a desire to "explore possibilities." Only 11% indicated that their primary motivation for establishing an online edition was to "make money." At the same time, nonprint media, especially magazines and television stations, were establishing their own web presence.

Chyi and Sylvie (1998) identified four submarkets within which electronic newspapers compete: local information, long-distance information, local advertising, and long-distance advertising. They also identified two areas in which product differentiation is essential: differentiation from traditional media through interactivity and features such as large databases, use of hypertext, and multimedia content; and differentiation from other online news sites through content.

It is in this competitive technological arena that media consolidation begins to create competitive advantages. First, group ownership allows the cost of developing the technology and software required for more sophisticated sites to be amortized over a number of newspapers or stations, reducing barriers to entry and allowing a more highly differentiated product. This advantage is further leveraged when multiple media groups create a joint venture to explore or develop a technology that might be too speculative or expensive for any of the groups alone. This provides a significant competitive advantage to group-owned versus individually operated media outlets.

Within the four competitive markets, consolidation provides additional advantages. Greater technological sophistication provides some advantage within local information and advertising markets because of the greater variety of online products that can be offered. Centrally developed sales and marketing plans can offer additional advantages. It is, however, in the long-distance information and advertising arenas that consolidation packs its greatest punch. The aggregation of information gathered by all members of a group in a format that is accessible or incorporated within each site can provide a depth with which the individual site operator cannot economically compete, particularly in the areas of feature or analytical information. In the long-distance advertising market, consolidation offers the opportunity for the creation of national networks available to advertisers as a one-stop buy and consolidated sales resource.

In the local news market, where the advantages of consolidation are least, there are signs that strategic alliances may develop as an alternative. In the San Francisco Bay area, two strategic alliances have developed between newspapers and local broadcast outlets that involve the sharing of content (Hilts, 1998). In the first, the San Francisco *Chronicle* and *Examiner* newspapers joined with the local NBC affiliate. In the second, the San Jose *Mercury News* and Contra Costa Newspapers, both Knight-Ridder subsidiaries, have formed a similar cross-marketing alliance with the local CBS affiliate. The partnership provides broadcast previews of the newspapers' next-day headlines and newspaper staff appearances on some newscasts. In exchange, the television station provides video clips to enhance the newspapers' online sites. As yet, the exchange is focused on leveraging and sharing content only.

This sharing of content to improve competitive differentiation and minimize operating costs becomes particularly attractive if the operating environment is that of a transnational media conglomerate, where there is a richer variety of resources and a strategic philosophy of leveraging across product lines. It appears entirely possible that as the size and importance of the online audience grows, the ability to obtain highly differentiated content at minimized cost could become an increasingly important competitive advantage and provide further stimulus for concentration within ever-larger and more diversified media conglomerates.

LIMITATIONS

Exploratory in nature, this study has several limitations. The most obvious is the relatively limited sample size of eight U.S.-based firms. The primary data sources were 10-K reports filed with the Securities and Exchange Commission. This limited the possible pool of companies to publicly held U.S. firms because foreign firms, even if registered in U.S. securities markets, are not required to provide the same level of detailed information in their 8-K filings.

Some inconsistencies exist between the reporting procedures and financial data provided by companies in their 10-K filings and, over the period studied, variations in accounting methods and reporting formats occurred within the reports for individual firms, creating some difficulties in ensuring that the data used were truly comparable. Because most of the companies are engaged in both media and nonmedia activities and profit and loss data were not consistently available by business segments, the findings are somewhat affected by the results of nonmedia economic activity. Additionally, reliable information regarding acquisitions and sales of properties were not available for all companies for all years.

Finally, the period covered (1993–1999) reflects the initial blossoming of the World Wide Web as a platform for news and information delivery but fails to adequately reflect the long-term impact of many trends in technological convergence that are only beginning to emerge.

THE COMPANIES

Financial data from eight media-intensive companies were selected for analysis. The companies were:

• *Gannett Co.:* Gannett publishes newspapers, operates broadcasting stations, and is engaged in marketing, commercial printing, a newswire service, data services, and news programming. Headquartered in Arlington, VA, Gannett has operations in 43 states, the District of Columbia, Guam, the United Kingdom, Belgium, Germany, Italy and Hong Kong. It is the United States' largest newspaper group in terms of circulation, with 99 daily newspapers aggregating a combined daily paid circulation of 7.8 million. The company owns and operates 22 television stations, covering 17.5% of the United States.

• *The Washington Post Company:* Headquartered in Washington, DC, The Washington Post Company is engaged in newspaper publishing, on-line publishing, television broadcasting, the ownership and operation of cable television systems, magazine publishing, and the provision of educational services. It owns and operates 3 daily and 49 other newspapers (including the *Washington Post*) and 6 network-affiliated television stations, publishes *Newsweek* magazine and certain controlled-circulation trade periodicals, and owns and operates Kaplan, Inc., a leader in educational test preparation. Its foreign operations are primarily due to the publication of international editions of *Newsweek* and account for less than 5% of the company's consolidated revenues.

• *The New York Times Company:* The New York Times Co.'s holdings include newspapers, television and radio stations, magazines, electronic information and publishing, Internet businesses, and forest products investments. It owns and operates 17 daily newspapers, newspaper distribution services, news and features syndicates, 8 television stations, 2 radio stations, 4 golf-oriented general circulation magazines, a variety of general news and niche-oriented on-line services, and minority interests in a newsprint company.

• *Tribune Company:* Tribune Company is engaged in the publishing of newspapers, books, educational materials, and information in print and digital formats, and the broadcasting, development, and distribution of information and entertainment principally in metropolitan areas in the United States. The company owns the *Chicago Tribune* and three other major dailies with a combined average circulation of approximately 1.2

million daily and 1.9 million Sunday. It also owns entertainment listings, a newspaper syndication and media marketing company, a Chicago-area cable television news channel, and other publishing-related businesses. It operates Internet sites for its newspapers, 22 television stations, and 4 radio stations, and develops new online products and services. It also operates weekly publications, syndication activities, advertising placement services, entertainment listings, and other online-related businesses, as well as cable television news programming. The company's educational division develops supplemental and core curriculum materials for kindergarten through grade 12 in language arts, math, health and science, foreign language, and social studies. The company also owns the Chicago Cubs baseball team.

• *CBS/Westinghouse Corporation:* CBS Corporation reinvented itself between its 1995 acquisition of the CBS television network and the 1999 disposal of the last of the industrial business segments owned under the former corporate name of Westinghouse. It is now one of the largest radio and television broadcasters in the United States, and operates the largest outdoor advertising business in North America. It operates primarily in the United States and owns and operates 16 television stations that are integrated into its network and syndication operations that produce and distribute news, public affairs, entertainment, and sports programming to more than 200 television stations and other outlets. Through Infinity Broadcasting, it operates 162 radio stations and the largest outdoor advertising businesses in North America. It also operates several cable television networks, including The Nashville Network (TNN), Country Music Television (CMT), and two regional sports networks. The company also operates Internet sites related to its cable and broadcast components.

• *Viacom Inc.:* Viacom Inc. classifies its global operations into six business segments. The networks segment operates cable television networks including MTV, Showtime, Nikelodeon, Nick At Night, VH1 Music First, and TV Land. The entertainment segment includes Paramount Pictures, Paramount Television, and Paramount Stations Group. Paramount Stations Group operates or programs 19 broadcast television stations. The entertainment segment also includes motion picture and music publishing operations. The video segment consists of an approximately 82% interest in Blockbuster, which operates and franchises video stores worldwide. The parks segment, Paramount Parks, owns and operates six theme parks in the United States and Canada. The publishing segment publishes books and related multimedia products under such imprints as Simon & Schuster, Pocket Books, Scribner, and The Free Press. The online segment provides online music and entertainment, information, community tools, and e-commerce through Internet sites related to MTV, Nickelodeon/Nick At Night, and VH1 Music First. In May 2000, Viacom acquired CBS.

• *Time Warner Inc.:* Time Warner Inc. classifies its business interests into six segments. Cable networks consist principally of interests in domestic and international basic cable networks and pay television programming services and the operation of World Championship Wrestling and sports franchises. Basic components include the Turner Networks, the CNN family of channels, HBO, and Cinemax, as well as advertiser-supported online sites. Publishing consisting principally of interests in magazine publishing (including *Time, Sports Illustrated, People, Fortune, Life,* and a number of specialized or regional publications), book publishing (Time-Life Books, Warner Books, Brown Little, and Oxmore House), and direct marketing (Time-Life products and Book-Of-The-Month Club). The music segment consists primarily of interests in recorded music and music publishing. Principle record labels in the United States include Warner Bros., and Atlantic. The Warner Music International division operates through subsidiaries and affiliates and their licensees in 67 countries. Filmed entertainment subsidiaries produce and distribute theatrical motion pictures, television shows, animation, and other programming; produce and distribute related home video products; operate the WB Television Network; license rights to the company's characters; operate retail stores featuring consumer products based on these characters and brands; and operate motion picture theaters. Comic books and theme parks operated in Germany, Spain, Australia, the United States, and Central and South America are also included in the entertainment segment. The cable segment consists of interests in cable television systems serving 12.8 million customers in 1999. Digital Media consists of interests in Internet-related and digital media businesses.

• *The Walt Disney Company*: The Walt Disney Company classifies its worldwide operations in five business segments. Media networks include radio, television, and cable operations. Disney owns and operates 15 broadcast television stations, the ABC Television Network (which has 225 affiliated stations), 50 radio stations, and ABC Radio NETworks (which provides programming to 4,500 affiliated stations). The company also owns or has significant investment in foreign and domestic cable channels including the Disney Channel, Toon Disney, SoapNet, ESPN, A&E Television Networks, Lifetime Entertainment Services, and E! Entertainment Television. The studio entertainment segment produces motion pictures, television programs, musical recordings, and live stage plays. The company also produces and distributes home audio and video products and a monthly general interest magazine. The parks and resorts segment operates Disney resorts in Florida and California and receives revenues from Disneyland Tokyo and Disneyland Paris. This division also includes a cruise line, a National Hockey League franchise, and a major league baseball franchise. The consumer products segment licenses the use of the company's characters for merchandise and publication. The Internet media business develops and distributes online content targeting consumer interests in sports, news, family, and entertainment. Sites include ABC.com, ABCNews.com, Disney.com,

ESPN.com, Family.com, and Movies.com. This segment also manages Disney websites devoted to e-commerce such as DisneyStore.com, DisneyVacations.com, ABC.com Store, ESPN Store Online, and NASCAR Store Online.

The data were examined from two perspectives—as a single group and as two groups based on their distribution of activities and revenues. For the latter analysis, the companies can be classified rather comfortably into two categories. Group 1 companies are those whose revenues have a heavy media component but whose activities tend to be more focused on content generation and distribution than on simple news. Companies in this category include Time-Warner, CBS, Viacom, and Disney. As a group, they tend to be more broadcast oriented than print focused.

Group 2 consists of media organizations that are primarily focused on newspaper publishing. This group includes the Tribune Company, The New York Times Company, Gannett Co., and The Washington Post Company. Although each of these groups has nonprint business operations, the majority of their revenues are dependent on newspapers and related services such as syndication and news services.

RESEARCH HYPOTHESES AND METHODOLOGY

The traditional behavior of media markets shows a clear tendency toward increased concentration as regulatory and economic barriers to entry decline. Economic theory predicts that, under such conditions, the least cost producer emerges as the economic winner and that the desire to gain the presumed efficiency advantages of increased concentration and opportunities for leveraging content encourage more concentration. Therefore:

> *Hypothesis 1*: Increased management efficiencies and greater margins can be realized as corporations become more concentrated within their core industries. Acquisition and merger activities that result in increased concentration within media will result in increased operational efficiencies.

Profit margins based on operating income as a percentage of revenue (pretax) were used as a measurement of operating efficiency. The diversity of SIC codes represented by businesses operated by the company were considered measures of concentration among business lines.

If time efficiencies are being achieved, these gains should be reflected in the organizations' labor efficiencies. It is to be expected that the degree of efficiencies that may be realized will vary from medium to medium, but that the opportunities for centralization and economies of scale will have a positive impact on all growing organizations.

> *Hypothesis 2*: The amount of time efficiency will vary by medium. Per-employee revenues for some media segments will be greater than for others.

FINDINGS

For the overall sample, operating margins were significantly and negatively correlated to the SIC diversity index ($-.557, p < .001, n = 64$). At the group level, the negative correlation between margins and SIC diversity was significant for Group 1 ($-.520, p = .005, n = 27$) but was not statistically significant for Group 2 ($-.308, p = .126, n = 26$). Regression analysis indicates that SIC diversity accounts for more than one fourth of the variance in margins for Group 1 ($R^2 = .27, t = -3.041, p = .005$).

Because Group 2 consists of primarily newspaper-oriented companies, its share of U.S. advertising expenditures offers another measure of operating efficiency. By this measure, there is a significant, positive correlation between SIC diversity and advertising share ($.471, p = .015, n = 26$). Regression indicates that SIC diversity accounts for almost one fourth of the variance in advertising market share held by the firms in Group 2 ($R^2 = .222, t = 2.615, p = .015$). These seemingly conflicting findings can be explained by comparing SIC diversity levels for Group 2 (mean = 3.85) with Group 1 (mean = 6.7). The differences are statistically significant ($t = 8.575, df = 51, p < .001$). For Group 2, SIC diversity primarily means diversity within advertising delivery platforms rather than across industrial segments.

Transactions (acquisitions/dispositions) activities appear to be different for Group 1 and Group 2 companies. There is a significant correlation between the level of transaction activities and the diversity of SIC codes for Group 1 companies ($.462, p = .04, n = 20$). The relationship between transactions and SIC diversity is not significantly correlated for Group 2 ($.130, p = .554, n = 23$), even though the mean number of transactions for Group 2 (6.91 per year) was nearly double the number for Group 1 (3.75). This indicates that Group 2 companies are more focused on increasing operating concentration in their existing industry segments, whereas Group 1 companies are more actively diversifying.

For the overall sample, operating margins were significantly and positively correlated to the companies transactions levels ($.387, p = .005, n = 50$). At the group level, the positive correlation between operating margins and the transactions index was not significant for Group 1 ($-.271, p = .247, n = 20$) but was significant for Group 2 ($.533, p = .009, n = 23$).

These findings generally support the first hypothesis. They indicate that the companies achieving the greatest efficiencies are those that seek to minimize and concentrate their range of industrial segments.

A t-test was used to compare the year-over-year percentage of operating income change for the two groups to identify differences between the groups based on type of media investment. The groups were not significantly different, indicating that operating income growth may be unrelated to the organization's type of media investment. Results were:

Group 1 ($n = 23$)
Group 2 ($n = 22$), $t = .968$ (df = 43, $p = .33$)
Means: Group 1 = .12; Group 2 = .14

When the groups are compared based on operating revenue per employee (a measure of operational efficiency that avoids some of the accounting complexities that can affect profitability calculations), Group 1 is significantly lower than Group 2. Regression indicates that group membership accounts for slightly more than one tenth of the variance in per-employee revenue for the companies in the sample ($R^2 = .112$, $t = 2.699$, $p = .009$).

Group 1 (n = 25)
Group 2 (n = 25), $t = 2.735$ (df = 48, $p = .009$)
Means: Group 1 = \$132,520; Group 2 = \$212,340

These results appear to support Hypothesis 2. There are significant differences between the media firms that are most concentrated in broadcast and content production (Group 1) and those that are most concentrated in newspaper production (Group 2).

CONCLUSIONS AND DISCUSSION

Although limited in scope, these preliminary findings show support for both research hypotheses and for the model of forces impacting media structure proposed earlier. Clearly, the benefits of economic convergence were limited during the period studied. Economic convergence, clearly a major strategic objective for Group 1 corporations, failed to achieve the level of efficiency demonstrated by Group 2 when viewed by revenue per employee measures. There are several possible explanations. Convergence as a business strategy is still very young. Both the skills of marketers and technological support and infrastructure are relatively unsophisticated but are rapidly improving. Both Disney and CBS/Westinghouse entered broadcasting during this period, and mergers of this magnitude—hampered by the inertia characteristic of all large organizations—take time to mesh smoothly. Another factor may lie in the variety of business segments involved. The findings indicate that there are clearly different time/efficiency requirements associated with different media, and this study did not attempt to measure or control for these variables.

The performance of Group 2 does provide evidence that focused expansion in a product-related business segment can pay dividends. For the primarily newspaper-oriented companies, expanding into advertising-related business lines where there is a common core of expertise resulted in increased market share and higher time/labor efficiencies. This implies that intra-industry concentration may, at least in the short term, offer greater efficiencies and more opportunities for economic convergence than does interindustry concentration.

More research is needed to precisely quantify the impact of convergence and concentration on these evolving media corporations. A larger, more global, and more detailed analysis of individual business lines within the companies should be conducted. This study focused on total revenues and profitability as measures of impact. Ultimately, if a convergence strategy is successful, those are the most relevant standards because economic benefits should accrue to all the company's business segments. If Disney builds features into one of its news sites to generate interest in its theme parks or feature films, for example, the results should be reflected in increased park and movie revenues. But more analysis of the varying labor requirements and economic performance of each media component of a converging company are critical to understanding the rapidly evolving global media industry.

REFERENCES

Bates, B. J. (1993). Concentration in local television markets. *Journal of Media Economics, 6*(3), 3–21.

Brodesser, C. (1997, May 5). A billion for billboards: Giant outdoor systems gets even bigger with deal for 3M unit. *MEDIAWEEK, 7*, p. 5.

Brown, S. (1998, February 2). Living large in 1997: TV, radio post records for multiples, broker involvement. *Broadcasting & Cable*, p. 32.

Busterna, J. (1991). Price discrimination as evidence of newspaper chain market power. *Journalism Quarterly, 68*, 5–14.

Chan-Olmsted, S. (1996). Market competition for cable television: Reexamining its horizontal mergers and industry concentration. *Journal of Media Economics, 9*(2), 25–41.

Chyi, H. I., & Sylvie, G. (1998). Competing with whom? Where? And how? A structural analysis of the electronic newspaper market. *Journal of Media Economics, 11*(2), 1–18.

Gershon, R. (1993). International deregulation and the rise of transnational media corporations. *Journal of Media Economics, 6*(2), 3–22.

Griswold, A. (1998). *Newspapers online: Finding new direction?* Unpublished manuscript, University of North Carolina at Chapel Hill.

Grossman, L. (1998). The death of radio reporting: Will TV be next? *Columbia Journalism Review, 37*(3), 61.

Hilts, E. (1998). San Francisco's latest media convergence. *Editor & Publisher, 131*(17), 40.

Lacy, S., Shaver, M. A., & St. Cyr, C. (1996). The effects of public ownership and newspaper competition on the financial performance of newspaper corporations: A replication and extension. *Journalism and Mass Communication Quarterly, 73*(2), 332–339.

Matthews, M. (1996). How public ownership affects publisher autonomy. *Journalism & Mass Communication Quarterly, 73*(2), 342–353.

McChesney, R. (1999). *The global media giants.* Retrieved February 3, 1999, from http://www.fair.org/extra/9711/gmg.html

McClellan, S. (1996, September 2). Staffs pay price for big-ticket mergers. *Broadcasting & Cable*, p. 14.

McKean, M., & Stone, V. (1992). Deregulation and competition: Explaining the absence of local broadcast news operations. *Journalism Quarterly, 69*(3), 713–723.

Middleberg, D., & Ross, S. (1999). *The Middleberg/Ross media in cyberspaces study 1997.* Retrieved January 28, 1999, from http://www.middleberg.com/studies/print/fulloverview.cfm

Picard, R. (1988). Measures of concentration in the daily newspaper industry. *Journal of Media Economics, 1*(1), 61–74.

Picard, R. (1994). Institutional ownership of publicly traded U.S. newspaper companies. *Journal of Media Economics, 7*(4), 49–64.

Powers, A. (1990). The changing market structure of local television news. *Journal of Media Economics, 3*(1), 37–55.

Rathbun, E. (1996, March 11). $8 Billion bull loose in station market. *Broadcasting & Cable,* p. 40.

Stempel, G., & Hargrove, T. (1996). Mass media audiences in a changing media Environment. *Journalism & Mass Communication Quarterly, 73*(3), 549–558.

Taylor, C. (1996, October 26). NAB: FCC's Ness addresses consolidation. *Billboard,* p. 86.

6

Time Management and CNN Strategies (1980–2000)[1]

Mercedes Medina
University of Navarra

Time constitutes a fundamental factor in the strategies of media companies. According to some studies, audiences are attracted to the media depending on their supply of time. For example, the management of television programming is conditioned by the viewer's time. Giving its time to media, the audience becomes powerful because the revenues of the commercial television companies depend on the audience's viewing. That is why media try to get more time from the audience. Time demanded by the media, especially for television, is leisure time. But the distribution of audience time depends on many factors apart from media supply, such as work, family and social activities, and even the weather. The media does not control these factors, but the media can influence the viewers. According to Beesley et al. (1996), the influence of media on the audience depends directly on the amount and quality of time devoted to media.

Consumption time is but one dimension considered in the management of media companies. There are other aspects such as production time, length of programs, commercial slots, prime-time and daytime programs,

[1]For questions, contact: Dra. Mercedes Medina, Departamento de Empresa Informativa, Facultad de Comunicación, Universidad de Navarra, 31080 Pamplona (ES). Phone: +34 948 42 56 55; e-mail: mmedina@unav.es

or time available for advertisers. Media owners have to make decisions about time availability and distribution. Usually, companies plan a strategy addressed to maximize resources in order to achieve specific objectives. A good strategy is often a long-term process. The short-term decisions become reactive tactics to changes in the market.

Having these concepts in mind, this chapter analyzes the strategy of the Cable News Network (CNN) from 1980 to 2000. One of the specific features of CNN that distinguishes it from other television channels is precisely the use of time. CNN's management views time in a different way compared to other media companies. Time in CNN is a business. It constitutes its identity. In this sense, time not only influences CNN's informative style, but also its management and strategies.

According to this time dimension, in this chapter I try to answer three questions about CNN. First, how does time influences CNN programming and its informative style? Second, how does CNN's international structure facilitate the use of time? Third, as a business, how has CNN diversified its activity along the time dimension? These aspects can be identified with three dimensions of time: informative time, which is related to the news coverage and broadcast transmission; international time, which relates to CNN's distribution all over the world and time-consumption issues; and historical and business time, which encompasses the evolution of the company and its adaptation to the industrial changes during the years.

TIME MANAGEMENT

CNN debuted in 1980, as an innovation of Ted Turner. After 20+ years, there are some aspects that have undergone change, but the original mission is still alive. Although Turner was criticized by both insiders and outsiders, his views about the demand for news was correct, and many competitors have followed suit. CNN based its channel on the need for information 24 hours per day, every day of the year. In Turner's own words, "On CNN news is the star" ("The CNN Story," 2001). Turner understood time as an added value to information. Thus, CNN can be studied from three different dimensions of related time: informative time, international time, and historical time.

Informative Time

Programming constitutes the supply of a television network. To talk about programming is to talk about time. Programming can be understood as the content delivered to the audience. Programming is also the activity of program distribution during the day according to target time slots. The available audience time for television consumption causes the traditional division between prime time and daytime. Programming has to be produced and edited at a certain time, and the duration of programs depends on time. Programming time is limited by broadcast time and coverage time.

Although television operates 24 hours a day, the fact is that the average audience member does not dedicate more than 3 or 4 hours per day to television consumption. This time is also concentrated at certain times of the day, typically *prime time*. It is "prime" because the best programming is presented then.

However, from the beginning CNN operated under different rules. Its programming was defined as 24 hours of international news, presented in flashes of 2½ minutes, broadcast in 30-minute intervals throughout the day. According to Wallis and Baran (1990), the immediate availability of CNN provided a maximum of information in a minimum time. CNN created what was called "the CNN factor" related to breaking news and direct information. Events that occurred in just about any place on earth were available for the audience at any time.

In this sense, it is possible to say that the CNN programming is not conditioned by time. The conventional outlines of dividing programming into daytime and prime time are not also taken into account in CNN newsroom decisions. As a senior international assignment editor said, "The hour changes depending on what time it is. It is always prime-time somewhere" (Flournoy & Stewart, 1997, p. 4). This shows how CNN production and editing time is simultaneous to programming time. The international coverage and news distribution link consumption time and broadcast time.

To cover 24 hours every day from all over the world, CNN needs more qualified employees than do other television channels. Continuous production of news is possible thanks to 4,000 employees in the form of journalists, producers, and technicians. They cover news around the world. CNN has a unique corporate culture in which all members work as a team (Flournoy & Stewart, 1997).

The training of news professionals is one of the most important objectives of CNN management, which instills a series of values and a common culture. According to Küng (2000), in CNN there is a relationship between culture and strategy. In an internal survey of CNN employees made by Lichter and Rothman in 1981, uniformity was detected in their views on society. Most employees considered that the goals American society should reach were: to maintain a stable economy and a high growth rate, to fight against crime, to ensure the internal defense, to obtain a more human and less impersonal society, to promote the participation of citizens in the decisions about their work and community, to make nicer cities, and to highlight the importance of work ideals (Volkmer, 1999).

Another practical decision related to employment at CNN was to attract professionals from other networks in order to build an international point of view to news coverage. Among those hired included Brent Sadler, the Middle East correspondent for Britain's Independent News (ITN); former ABC correspondent, Hilary Bowker; Richard Kaplan, a top ABC executive who was contracted as president of CNN/USA in August 1997. Other big names soon followed: In December 1997, ABC news correspondents Jeff Greenfield and Judd Rose were hired; and in January 1998 Tony Maddox, who had worked for BBC, was contracted as an editor and director of CNN International (Whittemore, 1990).

The last aspect of personnel policy influenced by the time factor is the work routines of professional journalists. Because there are time limitations, journalists have to make an effort to summarize the events and present the most relevant aspect of the news. This was a challenge for many journalists who were not used to such constraints (Zelizer, 1992). According to Volkmer (1999), "Journalists at a round-the-clock news operation have to be more alert, making sure that the facts are correct and making sure that the information that they are going to present is clear, because television and radio journalism goes by and you don't get it back" (p. 147).

The informative style of CNN programming differs from traditional programming in regard to how it values time. Despite the innovative style of CNN, some criticisms appeared of the way it presented news. The urgent need for actuality and instantaneous broadcasting eliminates reflection and contrast. A former employee for Headline News said, "I don't think that live availability always creates a positive situation. ... You have lost the time for measured thought" (Flournoy & Stewart, 1997, p. 62). If simultaneous information is more important than investigation, the viewer can lose the meaning of news (Wallis & Baran, 1990).

Some authors claim that news is created to move feelings rather to increase knowledge. García Avilés (1999), for example, argued that live coverage affects the emotions of the viewer. Colombo (1982) was concerned with the triviality of information on television. Volkmer (1999), quoting Robert Ross about the danger of live coverage, explained: "Live coverage eliminates the opportunity for editing and reduces the inclination for insertion of interpretative material. The viewer receives timely, first hand 'primary source,' rather than delayed, secondary, edited information" (p. 139).

CNN news is frequently criticized because of its neutral approach. Colombo (1997) compared the neutrality of CNN with the International Red Cross, a nonprofit company. Competitors of CNN attribute its reputation to its presentation of news in a fair and balanced way. The lack of ideological and political bias is seen by the competitors as an advantage to attract more viewers (Larson, 2000).

Furthermore, CNN is also criticized for giving a very narrow American focus to the news (Nobre-Correia, 1995). Tom Johnson, CNN president in 1996, said, "There was obviously a consciousness that you needed to be neutral in terms of reference to us as Americans" (Flournoy & Stewart, 1997, p. 127). Although CNN divided its services by regions, it did not always present the local view of topics, and it mainly covered news involving the United States. Wallis and Baran (1990) researched the coverage of selected news channels and demonstrated how CNN covered the United States more than it covered other countries (See Table 6.1.)

However, CNN is not the only service focused on the United States. As Table 6.1 illustrates, CBS also devoted 57% of its news time to news from the United States. On the other hand, the BBC devoted 24% of its time about UK

TABLE 6.1
News Coverage by Selected Services (Percentage Distribution
of Countries/Regions Reported)*

Area of coverage	CNN Headline News	CBS News	BBC World
USA	77%	57%	14%
Western Europe	4%	10%	9%
UK	2%	0.4%	24%
USSR	0.5%	3%	7%
China	0.5%	0%	0.6%
Japan	2%	0%	0.3%
Asia	3%	8%	9%
Australia	1%	1%	2%
South America	0.3%	0.4%	4.9%
Central America	2.7%	4.3%	1.8%
Eastern Europe	0.3%	0%	2.1%
Africa	0.8%	2.7%	7.0%
Middle East	5%	12%	13%

Note. From *The Known World of Broadcast News: International News and the Electronic Media* (p. 256), by R. Wallis and S. Baran, 1990, London: Routledge. Copyright © 1990 by Routledge. Reprinted with permission.
(*) Study of 9 programs between November 10 and 21, 1986.

news, and 14% to U.S. news. This suggests that it is easier for news services to cover domestic news than international news, and that the United States offers up a huge amount of information because of its size and international power.

In conclusion, the informative mission of CNN brings the channel toward an international dimension that is also facilitated by the use of time. One of its promoters expressed this idea in the following words: "Creating news programs that are compelling and relevant to a global audience means that CNN must report on important events whenever and wherever they happen. In doing this, the network continues to expand as a global communicator" (Flournoy & Stewart, 1997, p. 209).

International Time

Not satisfied with just CNN and CNN Headline News, Turner Broadcasting Services launched CNN International (CNNI) in 1985. CNN International was created to build more of an international audience. The number of households receiving CNN channels grew steadily, as shown in Table 6.2.

In 1991, CNN and Headline News reached more than 100 million U.S. households; by 1995 that number had grown to over 126 million. CNN International also experienced rapid growth. By 1999, CNN International reached over 151,000 households.

Since 1997, CNNI segmented into four separate regional channels: Europe/Middle East and Africa, Asia/Pacific, Latin America, and U.S. The Europe/Middle East and Africa covered 33 countries with 40 hours of programming originating from the London production center. In Asia, CNNI serves 29 countries; although the programs are produced in English, they are also dubbed into local languages. CNNI has served Latin America since 1980, but since 1989 it covers the entire region in English. Table 6.3 documents the worldwide coverage of CNNI.

CNN's international distribution is based on a double strategy of establishing bureaus outside the United States and signing alliances and joint ventures with other companies in different national markets. CNN builds its relationships with other companies by inviting local stations around the world to submit stories to its global "World Report" newscast. According to Flournoy and Stewart (1997), this business practice enabled a diverse

TABLE 6.2
U.S. and International Coverage Households (in thousands)

	1991	*1992*	*1993*	*1994*	*1995*
CNN	58,877	61,172	62,420	62,738	67,244
CNN Headline News	48,223	51,354	54,219	54,191	59,326
Total U.S. households covered	107,100	112,526	116,639	116,929	126,570
CNN International households	15,500	34,700	45,100	57,392	71,381

Source: Turner Broadcasting System. Inc., *Annual Report* (1993), p. 23; (1995), p. 28.

TABLE 6.3
CNNI Worldwide Coverage Households (1999, in millions)

Area	*Households*
Europe/Middle East/Africa	107.2
Asia/Pacific	25.0
CNNI U.S.	11.6
Latin America	7.7

Source: CNN Press Release (1999, May 4).

group of media to be part of the CNN family. By 1999, CNN was available in 212 countries and territories.[2]

The strategy of regionalizing global news helps CNN achieve its goal of obtaining information from any point of the world. Furthermore, it adds a local perspective that is important to local audiences (Whittemore, 1990). In Volkmer's words, "CNN keeps expanding internationally, and collaborating locally in order to gain local advertisers and explore new market niches, such as out-of-home markets, and customize news markets by using the local languages (Volkmer, 1999, p. 134).

Flournoy and Stewart (1997) summarized four aspects of the strategy used to internationalize CNN: to contract multicultural personnel; to build an international reputation of fairness, justice, and sensitivity toward local points of view; to develop programs to teach and train local professionals and to elaborate an international protocol; and to establish international relations and contracts. In fact, this strategy is possible thanks to CNN's original concept of being a 24-hour information channel for the world.

CNN has sought to improve its credibility among international audiences and local foreign companies. CNN earned a reputation among international media companies through its "links to national media and power elite secured privileged access to domestic sources, building agency credibility for world markets" (Boyd-Barret, 1997, p. 136). CNN's international reputation helped the network to achieve an influential position among its partners.

In summary, the founders of CNN thought that it was necessary to reach an international audience, to increase the production of news reports, to achieve prestige and to increase subscription revenues. In the 1980s, some observers believed there was little international demand for international news. However as Hoskins, McFadyen, and Finn (1997) pointed out, "CNN and the BCC World Service have demonstrated that a significant global market segment is willing to watch foreign-based international news" (p. 147). The success of CNN was due to the increases in the number of subscribing households both inside and outside the United States, and to the international alliances with local broadcasters and satellite and cable operators.

However, the key question that responds to the real demand for news is not how many households receive CNN, but how many people watch CNN and how much time they spend with the channel. Although the number of U.S. households subscribing to CNN increased from 1990 to 1995, CNN's ratings actually decreased. In 1991, CNN's U.S. ratings reached 1.2, but by 1995 it had decreased to 0.9 (a U.S. rating is 98 million television households).

Although humans have a need to be informed, the means to satisfy this need and the selection of the events that are important to citizens are not so clear. Curiously, CNN obtains its highest ratings when international disasters or controversial events occur (Kloer & Kempner, 2000). *Broadcasting & Cable* (McAdams, 1999) pointed out that "people come to CNN when airplanes plummet, nations crash or disasters strike. When calm prevails, they

---

[2]CNN, *The CNN News Group* (1999, December).

leave again" (p. 45). According to Wisneck (1992), during the Gulf War over 200 local stations became new subscribers to CNN.

Table 6.4 shows the evolution of the CNN audience from 1991 to 1995. It is significant that the years when it reached its highest ratings coincided with two newsworthy events: the Persian Gulf War in 1991, and the trial of O.J. Simpson in 1995. It is difficult for CNN to maintain its audience when nothing special happens. When no disaster occurs, the average U.S. viewing remains between 300,000 and 500,000 viewers (Blumenthal & Goodenough, 1998).

It is interesting to compare the audience of earlier years with the audience of later events. For example, when John F. Kennedy, Jr.'s plane was reported missing in July 1999, CNN generated a 5.3 cable rating and 4.1. U.S. rating. The October 2000 Presidential debates garnered a 2.6 rating and delivered 2,066,000 households and 2,829 total viewers.[3]

Generally speaking, CNN's ratings for both CNN and CNN Headline news are not high compared to other cable networks in the U.S. television viewing market. Likewise, CNNI's audience is also small. According to Cohen, Levy, Roeh, & Gurevith (1996), "CNNI can be seen in only 1% of all households worldwide. While 1% of the globe's total population is most certainly a very large audience, there is little evidence to suggest that many of these potential CNNI viewers tune in" (p. 151).

In a 1995 survey directed by the Center for International Strategy, Technology and Policy in France, Germany, Italy, Netherlands, Norway, and the United Kingdom, respondents indicated that the European audience did not devote the same time to CNN as to other television channels. About 30.6% of those surveyed watched CNN between 5 and 7 days a week, 24.6% watched it 3 or 4 days a week, 17.1% watched it 1 or 2 days a week, and 22.4% watched it once a month (Flournoy & Stewart, 1997).

As discussed earlier in this chapter, CNN does not differentiate between daytime and prime-time programming. During prime time, viewing levels

TABLE 6.4
Average U.S. Viewing* and Average U.S. Rating (Household
in thousands/percentage of TV households)

Average Audience	1991	1992	1993	1994	1995
CNN	685/1.2%	400/0.7%	369/0.6%	361/0.6%	580/0.9%
Headline News	182/0.4%	172/0.3%	181/0.3%	166/0.3%	182/0.3%

*"Average U.S. viewing households" represents the average number of viewing households for the respective service at any time based on an average for each 24-hour period in the 12 rating periods in each indicated year.
Source: Turner Broadcasting System Inc. (1995), p. 28.

---

[3]CNN is most-watched cable news channel for presidential debates. (2000, October 18). http://cgi.timewarner.com/

on traditional networks and other entertainment services often outpace CNN unless there are significant news events. CNN viewers are not conditioned to the same type of program schedule on the other networks. One study of CNN viewers found that 60% of the audience paid attention for only 5 or fewer minutes (Flournoy, 1992). The paradox, then, remains not only in the scarce amount of time its audience dedicates to the channel, but also in the intensity (or lack thereof) of attention given.

However, this does not seem to be a concern for CNN. To attract the attention of those who can influence the world is more important for CNN than to achieve a huge number of viewers. CNN's audience profile consists of better-educated viewers, with high income and a particular interest in news (Volkmer, 1999). A European Marketing Survey (Media and Marketing Europe, 2001) found that CNN reached nearly 39% of Europe's high earners and opinion makers.

Historical and Business Time

CNN became profitable in 1985. Respecting the fundamental mission established by its creators (Turner first, followed by Time Warner in 1996 and AOL Time Warner in 2000), all the owners pushed the CNN brand to meet new market demands. CNN's business strategy consists of five points: maintain an international dimension, continue technological innovation, be a leader in the information business, take advantage of the opportunities inside the market, communicate peace and justice and protect a free environment, and flee from conventionality (Flournoy & Stewart, 1997).

Although CNN's mission was clear from the beginning, it took 5 years to achieve financial profits. At the beginning, there were many doubts and uncertainties that the service would last even 6 months. CNN lost $24 million in 1981, caused by inefficient technical reception, a general disinterest in news programming, limited cable television penetration, and scarce financing.

CNN continued adapting its business to market changes and meet public needs. Every new business was launched respecting the CNN corporate identity as a news leader and pioneer, with the goal of serving the audience interests and assuming the market risks (Küng, 2000).

The desires of serving the audience and adapting to their informative time led to the 1982 launch of CNN Headline News as a complement to CNN. This was followed by the 1985 debut of CNN International, the 1991 launch of CNNI for Latin America, and the 1997 creation of *CNN en Español* for the Spanish-speaking audience.

CNN found other ways to extend its signature brand. In 1992, the CNN Airport Network debuted to reach the "inactive" time of airline passengers while also promoting the regular CNN channel and generating potential subscribers. In fact, a high percentage of CNN subscribers usually tune in to the services when they stay in hotels while traveling. According to Flournoy and Stewart (1997), the Europe 2000 (EMS) survey, 22% of the respondents watched CNN in hotels. In another survey run by the Center for International Strategy, Technology and Policy (Georgia), 43.9% of the respondents declared that they watched CNN in their hotel rooms when they traveled, compared to 31.1% who watched at home and 23.7% who watched at work. As well, it was pointed out that 79.3% of the Europeans preferred hotels that subscribed to CNNI (Flournoy & Stewart, 1997).

Although CNN was a pioneer, competitors emerged. In 1982, ABC/Westinghouse launched Satellite News Channels (SNC). Turner eventually bought out the service when it failed to attract enough viewers to sustain advertising. CNN retained a monopoly on 24-hour news channels in the United States until 1996, when NBC and Fox launched CNBC and Fox News, respectively, and NBC formed a joint venture with Microsoft, MSNBC (McClellan & Brown, 1996). By the year 2000, CNN reached 77.8 million homes in the United States, MSNBC reached 54.6 million households, and Fox News reached 47.4 million (Heyboer, 2000). In Europe, competition started earlier. BBC World began in 1991, and Euronews started up in 1995. Both services attract fewer viewers than CNNI does.

The increasing competition from other news channels and the declining audience led CNN to diversify its content into new thematic areas, such as finance and sports. CNN discovered the growing interest of the audience for this kind of information. Finance became more important than general information because it was related to daily citizenship decisions (McAdams, 1999). On the other hand, sports can be considered as entertainment, and there was also an unsatisfied need in this field. In 1995, CNN founded CNNfn, specializing in business financial news and economic analysis, and in 1996 it created CNN/Sports Illustrated, a sports channel forged in partnership with the Time Warner-owned *Sports Illustrated* magazine.

With the development of the Internet, immediate information access was no longer an exclusive value of CNN. A competitive advantage of the Internet is the ability to reach audiences who speak a different language. Kloer and Kempner (2000) pointed out that although CNN is televised in four languages (English, Spanish, German, and Turkish), it already has websites in eight different languages (English, Spanish, Portuguese, Italian, Swedish, Danish, Norwegian, and Japanese).

However, CNN never viewed the Internet as a threat; instead, CNN considered it a challenge. In 1995, CNN Interactive was founded to explore the possibilities of new technologies. That year, CNN.com was launched, and in 1999 the business was further enhanced when CNN mobile was created. CNN websites have received over 4 billion hits since 1999, with an average of 550 million page hits a month since February 1999. On September 11, 1998, a record 34.26 million hits were recorded the day the independent counsel report of Kenneth Starr, detailing his investigation of former President Bill Clinton was posted (CNN, 1999).

In 2000 CNN.com expanded into CNN.com Europe to target the European audience. The European market presented a new challenge for CNN, as 20% to 30% of the 650 million CNN.com hits came from outside the United States.

CNN's interactive/Internet strategy can be summarized as follows. CNN wanted to use the Internet to help it continue to be the foremost provider of international news for the world; to attract the key opinion leaders; to be the channel where news is first broken, reported, and analyzed; to provide varied and innovative programming for a range of viewers around the world who take news and public affairs seriously; to regionalize its news services; to provide more focus and relevance; and to develop specific programming for the Asian, European, and Latin American markets. The new aspects were coherent with CNN's original commitment to develop new program formats and lengths to complement its existing services and to build viewer participation (Flournoy & Stewart, 1997).

Certainly, CNN management knew how to overcome difficulties and take advantage of the market challenges to develop new business, not only in the domestic market but also internationally. CNN has found great success in expanding on its signature brand. Because its supply was original, the audience response tended to be quick and successful. According to Tom Johnson, president and CEO of the CNN News Group, the history of the company can be divided into three ages separated by three milestones: the establishment of the 24-hour cable news service in 1980; the coverage of the Gulf War in 1990, and the competition of other international information distributors in 2000. In each age, CNN has been able to respond successfully to new risks by adapting to market conditions and building new business.

CONCLUSIONS

CNN has become an international force, not only for the viewers, but also for professional journalists and even for governments. Colombo (1997) commented about CNN's reputation: "There are not any mistakes in the programming, production, organization or technical aspects of this one of a kind news television. CNN deserves this recognition, say the experts, and it continues to practice a high level of journalism" (p. 190). Strobel (1996) pointed out the potential influence of CNN on international politics through its live coverage and public reactions to events. According to Cohen et al. (1996), "CNN has become the office intercom of the global elite" (p. 151). Sanders and Bale (1999) pointed out the influence of CNN among other news channels: "The morning work routine of the news director of Sky News includes, looking over the newspapers, headlines and CNN at 6:00 am" (p. 143).

Taking into account its geographical and consumption dimension, CNN has developed a news formula around the world to become an international business, as well to develop local businesses. This often happens when an international channel extends itself to another country, leading to an increase in local production. Euronews was impacted by CNN's influence. MacHill (1998) pointed out that "Euronews considers itself the European answer to CNN" (p. 429). Following CNN's strategy of regionalized broadcasts, in 1997 NBC opened a German "window" for Germany, Austria, and Switzerland households.

In its historical and business evolution, CNN has become one of the most prestigious brands among media companies within the information market. CNN's identity and prestige are based on its search for standards of balance, accuracy, and fairness. The image and prestige of its trademark give it power and a competitive advantage over other information sources. Hoskins et al. (1997) considered the challenges of a consolidated media company and used CNN as an example: "The most important implication is an increase in the power of established communication and entertainment brands or sources with a distinctive identity or brand equity relative to participants who lack any strong identity ... such as Disney, the BBC, CNN" (p. 141). On the other hand, Cairncross (1998) said "the specialized channels easily turn into commercial brands with all the expansion possibilities ... not many viewers declare [what] television they are going to watch ... that's when they tune into channels like CNN or MTV" (p. 106).

It is commonly accepted that people watch programs as opposed to channels. However, this is not the case with CNN. Tom Brooks, Lifetime Senior Vice President of Research, explained, "The networks have allowed cable to build these brands—Lifetime, Nick, CNN and Cartoon—and these brands are much stronger than shows" (McAdams, 2000, p. 20). Part of the reputation of CNN was devoted not to a huge audience, but to small audiences that were opinion leaders.

In conclusion, time has been a key factor in the management of CNN. In fact, CNN has based its strategy on a revolutionary concept of time. As outlined in this chapter, this time revolution was manifested in three aspects: programming, consumption, and business. The continuous programming allows CNN to have an international news flow and eliminates the concept of prime time. Consumption can occur on many different CNN brands, or via the Internet and mobile phone services. In terms of business, CNN learned how to adapt to new technologies and changing market needs. A strong strategy built on the original mission of serving audiences all over the world has been maintained over the years by CNN management.

CNN achieved international prestige and produced a revolution in news programming, precisely for its original conception of time viewing and broadcasting. CNN's approach to news and reality has influenced the communication field and the world. CNN is helping define the evolution of new technologies and the shift towards immediate access to information and entertainment (Loebbecke & Powell, 1998).

The Cable News Network faces a new challenge—whether to redefine its original distribution advantage through cable and satellite, or to distribute content through Internet. As Kloer and Kempner (2000) explained, "If the Internet continues a convergence with television and other media, the line between what is on the CNN cable network online is blurred." CNN knows how to cover news and attract viewers; how viewers obtain the news may be irrelevant as long as CNN maintains its brand and prestige.

REFERENCES

Beesley, M. E., Goyder, D., Matson, M. J., Sawers, D., Shew, W. B., & Stelzer, I. M. (Eds.). (1996). *Markets and the media competition, regulation and the interests of consumers.* London: IEA (The Institute of Economic Affairs).

Blumenthal, H., & Goodenough, O. (1998). *This business of television.* New York: Billboard Books.

Boyd-Barret, O. (1997). Global news wholesalers as agents of globalization. In A. Sreberny-Mohammadi, D. Winseck, J. McKenna, & O. Boyd-Barret (Eds.), *Media in global context, A reader* (pp. 131–144). London: Arnold.

Cairncross, F. (1998). *La muerte a distancia. Cómo la revolución de las comunicaciones cambiará la vida de la empresa.* Barcelona: Paidós.

CNN. (1999). *The history of CNN International 1985–1999.* Unpublished manuscript, Atlanta, CNN.

CNN Releases/News. (2000, October 18). *CNN is most-watched cable news channel for presidential debates.* Retrieved from http://cgi.timewarner.com

The CNN story: Great brand, dull TV. (2001, January 8). *Fortune,* pp. 39–40.

Cohen, A. A., Levy, M. R., Roeh, I., & Gurevith, M. (1996). *Global newsrooms, a study of the Eurovision news exchange local audiences.* London: John Libbey.

Colombo, F. (1982). *Televisión. La realidad como espectáculo.* Barcelona: Gustavo Gil.

Colombo, F. (1997). *Últimas noticias sobre el periodismo. Manual de periodismo internacional.* Barcelona: Anagrama, Colección Argumentos.

Flournoy, D. (1992). *CNN World Report. Ted Turner's international news corp.* London: John Libbey.

Flournoy, D., & Stewart, R. (1997). *CNN making news in the global market.* London: John Libbey.

García Avilés, J. A. (1999, December). La imagen totem: Algunas paradojas sobre los informativos en el final de milenio. *ZER,* pp. 131–146.

Heyboer, K. (2000, June). Cable clash. *American Journalism Review,* pp. 20–26.

Hoskins, C., McFadyen, S., & Finn, A. (1997). *Global television and film. An introduction to the economics of the business.* Oxford, UK: Oxford University Press.

Kloer, P., & Kempner, M. (2000, May 28). CNN at 20. Low ratings, unrest over merger, uncertain online future are unwanted guests at birthday party celebrating an amazing two decades. *The Atlanta Journal–Constitution* [Electronic version]. Retrieved April 30, 2001 from http://www.accessatlanta.com/partners/ajc/reports/cnn20/main/html

Küng, L. (2000). Exploring the link between culture and strategy in media organizations: The cases of BBC and CNN. *The International Journal on Media Management, 2*(2), 100–109.

Larson, M. (2000, November 6). Fox out the woods. *Mediaweek,* pp. 46–50.

Loebbecke, C., & Powell, P. (1998). Investigating the worth of Internet advertising. *International Journal of Information Management, 18*(3), 181–193.

MacHill, M. (1998). Euronews: The first European news channel as a case study for media industry development in Europe and for spectra of transnational journalism research. *Media, Culture and Society, 20,* 427–450.

McAdams, D. (1999, December 13). CNN stood up. Viewers fail to keep their appointment. *Broadcasting & Cable,* pp. 44–48.

McClellan, S., & Brown, R. (1996, June 24). Cable news prepares for war. MSNBC and Fox take different tacks as they get ready to battle CNN. *Broadcasting & Cable,* pp. 44–50.

Nobre-Correia, J. M. (1995). Une Europe quê te de médias europeéns. *Média Pouvoirs, 37,* 123–130.

Pan-European television. (2001). *Media and marketing Europe. The comprehensive guide to programming, distribution and viewership. 5th edition.* Pocket Guide.

Reinholz, M. (1999, November 10). The original hard sell cable networks use cross-media promotional campaigns to hype new shows. *Broadcasting & Cable,* p. 26.

Sanders, K., & Bale, T. (1999). Las actitudes profesionales de los periodistas británicos. *Comunicación y Sociedad, 12*(2), 135–156.

Strobel, P. (1996, May). The CNN effect. *American Journalism Review, 33*–37.

Time Warner Inc. (1996–2000). *Annual reports.* Retrieved October 28, 1999 from http://www.timewarner.com

Turner Broadcasting System, Inc. (1993). *Annual report.* Atlanta: Author.

Turner Broadcasting System, Inc. (1995). *Annual report pursuant to section 13 or 15(d) of the Securities Exchange Act of 1934.* Atlanta: Author.

Volkmer, I. (1999). *CNN. News in the global sphere. A study of CNN and its impact on global communication.* Luton, UK: University of Luton.

Wallis, R., & Baran, S. (1990). *The known world of broadcast news: International news and the electronic media.* London: Routledge.

Waterman, D., & Weiss, A. (1997). *Vertical integration in cable television.* Cambridge. MA: MIT Press.

Winseck, B. (1992). Golf war in the global village: CNN, democracy and the information age. In J. Wasko & V. Mosco (Eds.), *Democratic communication in the information age* (pp. 60–75). Toronto: Garamond.

Whittemore, H. (1990). *CNN: The inside story.* Boston: Little, Brown.

Zelizer, B. (1992). CNN, the Gulf War and journalistic practice. *Journal of Communication, 42*(1), 66–81.

7

Online, Time Is Money: Internet Growth and the Cost of Access in the United Kingdom and Europe[1]

David H. Goff
School of Mass Communication & Journalism,
University of Southern Mississippi

The World Wide Web is already an important tool of promotion and franchise extension for legacy media around the world. Streaming media technologies, somewhat crude in narrowband dial-up access mode, are forecast to enable delivery of full-motion digital video and audio when broadband connections to the Internet are more commonplace (Datamonitor, 1999). When the public commercial Internet emerged during the mid-1990s, the world's media and telecommunication systems were already engaged in a transformation from analog to digital technology. The rapid growth of the Internet accelerated this process and established the Internet's technical protocols as standards for virtually all digital networks. Soon, all media content will be deliverable through any digital connection; broadcasters, cable and DTH satellite television firms, telecoms, and joint ventures between

---

[1]For questions, contact: David H. Goff, Ph.D., University of Southern Mississippi, e-mail: david.goff@usm.edu

legacy and new media will compete for the attention of "media audiences" ("BBC fights," 1999; Goff, 2000). Observers worldwide view the 2000 merger between Internet access provider America Online (AOL) and media conglomerate Time Warner as a prototype for media firms in the coming broadband era.

LEGACY MEDIA, THE INTERNET, AND TIME

The business models of established electronic media have always been concerned with the number (and types) of people in the audience, and with the amount of time that audience members devote to specific media consumption. Such time has been measured for the purposes of making content decisions and justifying advertising rates, but never for the purpose of charging consumers directly for the net amount of time they spend consuming media content.

In the United States, the Internet followed this "free-to-air" approach because the telephone connection time needed for narrowband access to the Internet is not metered. Affordable personal computers, flat-rate unlimited access, and unmetered connection time combined with a strong economy in the late 1990s and early 2000s to power the Internet to phenomenal growth in the United States. In comparison, major European economies (the United Kingdom, France, Germany, Spain, and Italy) experienced much slower growth in numbers of Internet users. Furthermore, Europeans who venture online tend to spend far less time there than their American counterparts. As a result, Internet-related businesses have grown more slowly in Europe despite a rich economic environment. This has frustrated citizens, stymied media institutions eager to leverage their brand identities online, and thwarted the plans of businesses and governments intent on pursuing electronic commerce. The economic and political stakes associated with the growth of e-commerce are enormous. U.S. market research firm International Data Corporation (IDC) estimates that 15% of the world's population will be online by 2005, generating $5 trillion in Internet commerce (Owens, 2001a). European leaders want this prediction to come true, and to position their countries to gain a significant share of the expected revenues.

In Europe, until the late 1990s, computers were seldom sold at discount and Internet access subscriptions only added to the high cost of going online. However, the major impediment to Internet growth in Europe was the fact that, when online, connection time was metered by the local telephone company, usually a recently privatized national telephone service. The cost of connection time forced Internet users to log on for short intervals or to limit access to periods of lowest telephone rates. When consumers pay prohibitive charges for the time they spend online, e-commerce and the growth of all business models that rely on the Internet suffer (Ni hEildhe, 1999b).

This chapter examines the economic factors affecting the amount of time Internet users in the United Kingdom and other European countries spend online. The study first recounts the role of Internet service providers (ISPs) offering free Internet access in markets where network access is controlled by national telephone companies. Starting in late 1998, free ISPs stimulated rapid growth in the number of Internet users in the United Kingdom, and the phenomenon quickly spread to much of Europe (Rohde, 1999). Despite swelling the ranks of Internet users, free ISPs achieved only limited direct success in increasing the amount of time European subscribers spent online. However, the multitudes of new Internet users brought online by the free ISPs created enormous marketplace pressure for unlimited access plans and the provision of faster access technologies. In response, European national and pan-national governmental agencies intent on deregulating telecommunication industries began to accelerate the deregulatory process. The subsequent interplay of telecom and Internet access firms, government, and the public has yielded mixed results in terms of actual deregulation of dominant telecoms. Increasing time spent online requires the availability of either narrowband flat-rate or broadband access, alternatives that continue to be controlled by the former national telecoms. This chapter concludes with a assessment of the stratification of European Internet access markets, and the implications for media and e-commerce.

FREESERVE: THE FREE ISP PHENOMENON SWEEPS THE UNITED KINGDOM

The concept of free Internet service emerged with little fanfare in Europe, with the introduction of Mannesmann's Germany.net service in 1995 (Borzo, 1999). However, the September 1998 introduction of Freeserve in the United Kingdom by electronics retailer Dixons Group PLC launched a phenomenon that transformed the economics of Internet access in Britain and spread quickly to the continent. Dixons, the leading personal computer vendor in the United Kingdom, wanted to create an online presence for e-commerce and at the same time establish a British ISP as a lower-priced alternative to the U.S.-owned AOL-U.K. online service. As it explored ways to provide cheap access, Dixons discovered that it actually could offer Internet connections at no cost and still make money. British telecommunication regulation requires the telephone companies from which calls originate to pay a percentage of the interconnection revenues to the companies that terminate the same calls. Dixons Group contracted with the independent U.K. telecom, Energis, to receive the telephone traffic generated by Freeserve customers, in exchange for 40% of the telephone tariff revenue (Nairn, 1999; Tomlinson, 1999). Under the plan, most of this revenue reverted to an Energis subsidiary, Planet Online, the firm that provided the actual Internet services, including access. Freeserve's final share of the telephone connection revenue was approximately 4% (Nairn, 1999). In addition, Freeserve (and other free ISPs) charged customers an average of £1 per minute for providing online help (Kane, 1999).

By March 1999, 6 months after its launch, Freeserve PLC had become the largest ISP in Britain, with 1.3 million users and a 40% market share (Borzo,

1999; Trager, 1999). The NOP Research Group estimated an overall 48% increase in the number of British adults using the Internet during 1998 (compared with 1997), and growth in the number of home Internet users went from 3.4 million in December 1997 to 6 million in December 1998; Most of these gains were attributed to Freeserve ("More Than," 1999). Dixons effectively used its network of 1,000 retail stores to market Freeserve, and its first mover advantage proved to be valuable as hundreds of Freeserve imitators were quickly established by computer makers, grocery chains, newspapers, banks, other retailers, and even the BBC (Rohde, 1999). Free ISPs flourished despite persistent quality of service problems, including frequent busy signals and demand-related outages. Customer loyalty proved to be fleeting, as customers switched to new services or simply opened multiple accounts. Many even maintained paid Internet access services while signing up with free ISPs. Fletcher Research found that paid access services were more often used for e-mail, chat, and accessing premium content, whereas free ISPs were used for general Web surfing ("U.K. ISP Audience," 1999).

Internet competition in Britain evolved quickly during 1999. Many of the existing paid-subscription ISPs launched free services in an effort to retain market share. British Telecom (BT) launched a free service called BT Click+ (Berendt, 1999). AOL-U.K. responded with its own version of a free ISP, called Netscape Online. The most unusual competitor actually paid customers to surf the Internet. The firm's software displayed an adbar window and tracked the websites visited and the search terms used by its customers ("Sharkhunt.com," 1999). By the end of 1999, over 400 providers of free Internet service were operating in the United Kingdom, and the free ISP phenomenon had spread to most of continental Europe (Borzo, 1999).

THE FREE ISP MOVEMENT ON THE CONTINENT

Free ISPs attracted throngs of new Internet users in all parts of Europe. Table 7.1 summarizes available data on net changes after 1998, in numbers of Internet users. Within the European Union and Switzerland, some 2,000 free ISPs were operating by the end of 1999. Numbers of Internet users in these countries were estimated to have increased from 35 million at the end of 1998 to 45 million 1 year later, with 7.5 million of the new recruits attracted by free Internet access (Borzo, 1999). However, the market share of free ISPs varied from country the country.

Following introduction in Italy in early 1999, the free ISPs operated by Telecom Italia, Infostrada, and Tiscali secured 4 million customers, for an 80% market share (Rudiez, 2000). Forrester Research reported that by mid-summer 54% of Internet users in Sweden were free ISP customers. In Holland, the figure was 37% (Borzo, 1999). By late summer, the free ISP phenomenon reached central Europe (Gatsoulis, 1999). A June 1999 study by Benchmark Group reported that seven free ISPs had signed up 220,000 customers in France during the previous 2 months, and estimated that of this number 75,000 were new Internet users ("220,000 French," 1999). Overall, the number of Internet users in France increased 47% during 1999,

TABLE 7.1
Internet Growth in Europe: 1998–2000/2001
(number/population percentage/month)

Country	1998	2000/2001
Austria	442K/5.5%/August	3.0M/36.9%/October 00
Belgium	430K/4.2%/November	2.7M/26.4%/September 00
Denmark	1.1M/22.0%/November	2.9M/54.7%/July 01
Finland	1.4M/27.9%/August	2.3M/43.9%/August 00
France	2.5M/4.2%/May	11.7M/19.7%/August 01
Germany	7.3M/8.7%/October	28.6M/34.5%/August 01
Italy	2.6M/4.1%/May	19.3M/33.4%/August 01
Norway	1.0M/22.7%/December	2.5M/54.4%/July 01
Spain	2.4M/7.1%/November	7.4M/18.4%/July 01
Sweden	2.9M/33.0%/November	5.6M/63.6%/November 00
United Kingdom	7.5M/16.0%/October	33.0M/55.3%/June 01

How many online (Europe). (2001). *Nua Internet Surveys.* Retrieved November 8, 2001, from http://www.nua.ie/surveys/how_many_online/europe.html (Compiled November 8, 2001).

according to NOP Research ("France No Longer," 2000). In Spain, free ISPs began as regional services, but the concept spread quickly throughout the country, garnering nearly a half-million customers between June and August 1999. The Association de Usuarios de Internet estimated that free ISPs in Spain added 20% more Internet users in their first 10 months of operation (Rudiez, 2000).

However, in both France and Spain, the dominant ISPs are owned by the national telephone companies and their services are not free. Wanadoo, France Telecom's ISP, boasts over 750,000 subscribers; Ole, the top ISP in Spain, was acquired by Telefonica during 1998 (Tomlinson, 1999). The same is true in Germany where the free service Germany.net is the number three ISP. The market leaders—Deutsche Telekom's T-Online service (with 56% of the market) and AOL—both charge for subscriptions (Rudiez, 2000). Like other European economies, Germany experienced huge growth (53%) in Internet penetration during 1999 ("German Household," 2000).

ASSESSING THE EARLY IMPACT OF THE FREE ISP MOVEMENT

IDC described the free ISP phenomenon as "a critical milestone on the path of the emerging Internet economy" ("Flat-Rate," 1999). In the short term, the creation of the free ISP "solved" one of the three vexing problems of slow European Internet growth and contributed significantly to the solution of the remaining two. The free ISP phenomenon practically eliminated the cost of basic Internet access. At the same time, the ensuing competition among ISPs and the growing numbers of new Internet users contributed to greater price competition in the personal computer market. However, it is likely that the most significant impact of the free ISP concept in Europe will be its contribution to the resolution of the thorniest Internet growth deterrent: the cost of telephone connection charges.

EUROPEAN TELEPHONE TARIFFS, AND THE QUEST
FOR UNMETERED INTERNET ACCESS

In most European countries, the dominant telephone company was once the sole telephone company and was government owned. The standard business model involved cross-subsidies, and all calls were metered. Privatization of European telecoms began in the United Kingdom in the early 1980s, but real competition did not begin there until 1997 (Malim, 1999). The other major European nations instituted privatization and deregulation of the telecommunication sector by the end of 1998 ("Telecom Titans," 1999). Nonetheless, the former national telecoms remain the dominant firms in each country, with the government retaining majority ownership.

Deregulation forced former national telecoms like BT, France Telecom, Deutsche Telecom, and Telefonica into costly price competition for long distance and international business, effectively ending the use of profits from these lucrative areas to subsidize the cost of local service. Furthermore, because of their ownership of customer access networks (the "last mile"), Europe's major telecoms quickly established themselves as the primary means of connecting to the Internet. Most charged a flat rate for simple Internet access while collecting metered charges for every minute both business and residential customers spent online ("Battle for the Internet," 2000a; Essick, 1998). The revenue generated by customers' Internet access provided a windfall of profit that these firms needed badly as they restructured tariffs, faced new competitors, and invested in new technologies.

By luring customers away from the paid subscription services of the national telecoms, the upstart free ISPs introduced yet another dimension of competition, forcing the telecoms to respond or risk losing market share to new competitors. Furthermore, as free ISPs increased the number of Internet users, they subsequently fueled the growing anger of the online community over the cost of telephone access. Frustrated citizens, the media, and a business community eager to harvest the fruits of the information economy brought pressure to bear on governments, and this pressure was subsequently applied to the telecoms. In the most extreme instances, boycotts of telecoms and ISPs swept Spain, Germany, France, Switzerland, and Greece during late 1998 and 1999, and actually achieved some success in lowering the cost of Internet access calls (Borzo, 1999; Essick, 1999).

The deregulation and privatization movements of the late 1990s were designed to open markets and introduce the benefits of competition (Goff, 1998, 2000). Metered local telephone access, once accepted as necessary for the economic stability of the telecom industry, came under increasingly strident attack shortly after the emergence of Freeserve. Annual data from the Organization for Economic Cooperation and Development (OECD) revealed a strong correlation between the total cost of access and Internet growth. Reports noted the contrast between the high Internet penetration rates in low access-cost countries like the United States and Finland, and low penetration in high-cost countries like Germany (Essick, 1998). A January 1999 report from Datamonitor noted that online time was three times as expensive in the United Kingdom as in Nordic countries, and five times as expensive as in the United States. The U.K.-based Campaign for Unmetered Telecommunications called for a 24-hour-long pan-European Internet boycott to in support of flat-rate access (Ni hEilidhe, 1999a). The Office of Telecommunications (Oftel, the U.K. agency that regulates telecommunications) investigated the cost of calls to the Internet and noted that U.K. usage prices were actually above cost and that flat-rate unmetered Internet access for "high users" was economically feasible (Oftel, 1999).

Oftel's "raised eyebrow" and growing concern about extending the economic benefits of Internet access to British businesses led U.K. Chancellor of the Exchequer Gordon Brown to ask Oftel to advance a July 2001 deadline requiring BT to unbundle its local loop ("BT Fears," 2000). Data from the OECD showed the United Kingdom to be the sixth most expensive place in which to go online for 30 hours per month (OECD, 2000). In March 2000, British Prime Minister Tony Blair proposed initiatives aimed at providing low-cost universal Internet access by 2005 ("Tony Blair's," 2000). In April, the European Union's information commissioner echoed British efforts. In a speech in London, Erkki Liikanen proposed E.U. legislation intended to speed deregulation of the local loop throughout Europe. Liikanen recognized the importance of the Internet to consumers, but stressed the idea that European businesses were being denied significant cost savings achieved by online businesses in the United States and other parts of the world ("EU Drive," 2000).

One of the first efforts to quantify the restriction on Internet use attributed to telephone tariffs was provided by the British firm, Durlacher Research Ltd., in February 2000. The study supported the contention that metered local telephone access to the Internet was a significant deterrent to Internet use. Durlacher surveyed 4,000 U.K. households about Internet, mobile phone, and digital television use during the fourth quarter of 1999. Respondents with Internet access reported that online sessions lasted an average of 46 minutes. More important, respondents indicated that if telephone connection time were unmetered, the length of their Internet sessions would increase by over 100% and their frequency of access by 46%. The report projected that with unmetered telephone access, combined increases in frequency and Internet session length would triple residential Internet use from 130 hours to 386 hours per year (Durlacher Research Ltd., 2000).

The goal of offering unmetered narrowband access quickly became a high priority in the United Kingdom, especially for BT's competitors. However, actual delivery of unmetered service proved to be challenging. In March 2000, both Altavista-U.K. and the cable firm NTL announced plans to provide unmetered Internet access by the summer. Altavista planned to charge £35 to £50 initially, and then £10 per year. NTL's start-up price was to be £10, with customers required to spend £10 per month on NTL voice calls. BT responded with offers of two levels of unlimited access through a service called BT Surftime. When originally announced in December 1999, BT's proposed tariffs for unlimited access specified £13.98 for the weekend and evening off-peak periods, and £34.99 for full unlimited access ("BT Offers," 1999). Later, in response to the Altavista and NTL offers, BT promised customers unlimited access during weekends and evenings for £5.99 per month, or complete unlimited access for £19.99 ("The Cost of Connecting," 2000). Freeserve itself was forced to respond to these competitive pressures, announcing that £6.99 unlimited and unmetered access would be available by May 2000 ("Freeserve Unmetered Move," 2000).

The actual rollout of unmetered access in the United Kingdom was plagued with difficulties, again due to the control of the local loop by the former national telecom. BT made flat-rate Internet access available to its competitors, but required them to interconnect at the network level of the local exchanges, despite the fact that competing telecoms interconnect to BT at the higher-level main exchange. This arrangement forced competing ISPs to lease lines to the local exchanges from BT, and the use of these lines was metered (Harvey, 2000). Almost immediately, firms like Freeserve and Breathe.com experienced huge increases in access costs and growing losses as net surfers went online for extended sessions. Breathe.com experienced a doubling of time spent online by its unmetered access customers and even disconnected some of its heaviest users (Grande, 2000). By August, CallNet0800 and Line One had terminated their unmetered access services, and Altavista was forced to withdraw its unmetered access plan, despite having registered 250,000 prospects (Grande, 2000; Harvey, 2000). BT's practices led to complaints from the affected ISPs and other telecoms. Oftel responded with a series of studies and rulings that required BT to provide a solution called Flat Rate Internet Access Call Origination (FRIACO). This system involves the purchasing of access capacity rather than access time (Harvey, 2000).

By January 2001, unmetered access had achieved a degree of stability in the United Kingdom. With 2 million customers, Freeserve controlled a third of the market, charging £12.99 per month. AOL-UK (£14.99/month) entered the unmetered access competition in September 2000, but only after Oftel's FRIACO order reduced the cost of buying access from BT. British Telecom responded to these offers by lowering its unlimited access plan to £14.99.

The same pressures for cheap and unlimited Internet access were felt throughout the rest of Europe, but success in providing such service has been elusive. CyberCity began providing flat-rate services in Denmark in January 2000 and in Norway in March 2000 (Godell, 2000). In Spain, national telecom Telefonica's Telia service began discounting calls to the Internet in October 1999, and made flat-rate narrowband service available during mid-2000 (Battle for the Internet, 2000b; Nairn, 1999). By 2001, the Spanish government had forced Telefonica to allow other ISPs to connect to its network in order to market competing flat-rate access. However, policy enabled Telefonica to provide slow and unreliable connections to its competitors at noncompetitive prices (Hilburn, 2001).

AOL-Europe began offering unmetered access in France in late August, but the move was seen as a loss-leading effort to gain market share from France Telecom's Wanadoo service (Daniel & Grande, 2000). AOL-Europe also petitioned the German government to force Deutsche Telekom to lower the cost of local calls accessing the Internet (Baker, Echikson, & Robinson, 2000). AOL contended that a 20% to 50% reduction in charges for calls to the Internet would boost the German economy by 19 billion marks and create 400,000 jobs (Simpson, 2000). Deutsche Telekom announced its own plans to offer flat-rate Internet access from its T-Online service (and did so) by midsummer (Godell, 2000). However, by early 2001, both T-Online and AOL had cancelled their flat-rate plans. T-Online replaced flat-rate access with an array of plans providing either monthly allotments of 30 to 90 hours, or per-minute charges coupled to a monthly fee ("Telekom Scraps," 2001). The revised approach to narrowband access pricing by T-Online is viewed as a strategic move to attract more customers to the company's DSL broadband service (Cavallaro, 2001).

MOVING FORWARD: BROADBAND ACCESS, WIRELESS ACCESS, AND DIGITAL TELEVISION

While European ISPs were struggling to establish unmetered narrowband access in the second half of 2000, high-speed broadband Internet services were also being launched. At that time, only 0.2% of European households had broadband connections ("27 Million," 2000). Both wireline telecoms and cable companies are rolling out broadband capabilities, creating the potential for the "always on" Internet. Nonetheless, despite strong interest from consumers, the broadband access market in Europe experienced slower than expected early growth, and is predicted to achieve only 24.2% penetration by 2005, compared to 53.1% in North America ("Europe to Remain," 2001). Internet and personal computer penetration, availability of broadband technologies, competition, government policy, and general economic conditions vary widely across the region, resulting in significant variation in each country's broadband prospects. Germany, Denmark, the Netherlands, and the Nordic countries are predicted to outpace other European nations in broadband growth. By contrast, France, Spain, and Italy are expected to lag (eMarketer, 2001). The United Kingdom—the country with the most successful unmetered narrowband access market—ranks last among European nations in broadband households, with penetration not expected to top the 1% mark by the end of 2001 ("Europe to Remain," 2001).

Throughout Europe, telecoms are offering asymmetric digital subscriber line (ADSL) service using existing copper telephone lines. The pricing and installation of DSL service depends heavily on the policies of the dominant telecoms in each country. In the United Kingdom and other Western European countries, a shortage of DSL installation technicians hindered the initial rollout of broadband service. Competitors view this as a problem controlled by the dominant telecoms to their advantage ("Broadband Blues," 2001). Telecoms recognize that broadband market share is important to future prospects. However, because DSL broadband is substantially cheaper than fixed-line data connections for business customers, telecoms stand to lose significant revenue when business customers switch to DSL ("Broadband Blues," 2001).

Initially, British Telecom announced that it would make DSL available to competing ISPs at wholesale prices ranging from £40 to £150 per month for each connection, forcing the ISPs to either charge a higher rate to customers or subsidize the cost of service to subscribers (Nuttall, 1999). BT began rolling out its own BT Openworld DSL service in late 1999, initially charging £39.99 per month (Nuttall, 1999). FreeservePlus broadband service began in September 2000, acquiring its DSL access from BT. FreeservePlus charged £150 to set up a customer's service and £39.99 per month.

The cable industry's response to DSL is broadband access via cable modems. Obviously, this method of access is available only to households served by European cable firms, and the percentage of homes passed by cable varies widely among the nations of Europe. In contrast to the U.S. experience, the European cable industry was largely unsuccessful at building a market for multichannel television access during the 1980s. Present-day European cable firms are establishing themselves as competing suppliers of telephone service in addition to providing video services. Cable construction since the mid-1990s has been digital, and virtually all cable companies market Internet access. Like telecoms, cable companies realize the need to build their broadband market share. However, the cost of adding cable broadband Internet subscribers is high, and analysts point out that cable firms can make higher profits from selling premium television channels and video on demand to their video customers ("Broadband Blues," 2001).

Because European telecoms were slow to introduce broadband service, several international firms entered this market sector. The most significant, chello broadband, n.v., is owned by Amsterdam-based United Pan-European Communications n.v. (which is, in turn, owned by the U.S.

firm, UnitedGlobalCom, Inc.). With its own broadband IP backbone, chello offers European broadband services in the Netherlands, Belgium, France, Germany, Austria, Norway, and Sweden. The firm utilizes the full range of broadband delivery technologies rather than just DSL or cable (chello broadband, n.v., 2000). The future of companies like chello is uncertain, however. The company has succeeded in Europe because of the tentativeness of the former national telecoms in offering broadband. But, once the dominant telecoms complete the conversion of their networks to DSL capability, firms like chello may be crowded out. Analysts expect significant consolidation in the European Internet access market.

Mobile (wireless) telephony, already well established in Europe, has become a significant factor in both narrowband and broadband Internet access. Forrester Research estimated that there were 6.6 million wireless web users in Western Europe at the end of 2000, and projected that there would be more than 214 million by the end of 2004 (Williams, 2000). Wireless application protocol (WAP) received wide support among the world's major wireless equipment firms, enabling mobile phones, laptops, and palm computers to access the Internet from virtually anywhere in the world ("Tomorrow's Internet," 1999). Newer, faster, and higher bandwidth wireless technologies (e.g., i-mode, GPRS or General Packet Radio Service, and other 3-G or third-generation protocols) promise to expand the utility of the wireless Web.

IDC predicts that Western Europe will be home to nearly 80 million digital television subscribers by 2005 (Owens, 2001b). Near-universal availability of the Internet can be expected by 2010, if predictions about the diffusion of digital television are correct. By that time, many expect (or at least hope) that there will be little difference between television and the Internet in terms of video quality (Griffiths, 1999; Pringle, 2000). According to U.K. market research firm Ovum, digital television broadcasting "breaks down the barriers between the Internet, traditionally a telecommunications domain, and the traditional media-oriented television sector" ("Telcos and TV," 2000).

Digital television services are provided primarily by satellite broadcasters, cable firms, and terrestrial broadcasters, but telcos are expected to become competitors. Digital technology enables improved image and sound quality, delivery of an increased number of television signals within the same amount of broadcast spectrum or bandwidth, and interactive capabilities. There is virtually no limit to the types of content that will be deliverable by digital television. Broadcast programming, video on demand, content navigation aids, and Web pages will all be part the digital television content mix. Moroney (1999), citing predictions from Ovum, contended that digital television can easily control the mass market for interactive content. Datamonitor acknowledged the expected future ubiquity of digital set ownership and the ease and speed of access offered by digital television, but took the view that TV-based access may have broadest appeal for lower socioeconomic groups that were disenfranchised by the expense of personal computer ownership (Morrell, 2000).

TIME SPENT ONLINE INCREASES WITH BROADBAND ACCESS

The addition of broadband to the choices available for Internet access is a crucial step in increasing the amount of time spent online. A study conducted by
chello broadband, n.v., comparing actual Internet usage in broadband and
narrowband households in Europe, reinforces the usage pasterns predicted
earlier. Durlacher Research had predicted that unmetered narrowband access
would increase frequency of Internet access by 46%, online session lengths
would increase by over 100%, and hours of residential use would triple from
130 to 386 hours per person. However, the Durlacher study did not address
broadband access. In the chello study, narrowband Internet users in the same
markets served by chello's broadband service averaged 36 hours per month
(432 hours per year) online. Broadband customers were online twice as long,
72 hours per month (864 hours/year). Furthermore, broadband customers averaged four connections per day, twice the number of narrowband users
("chello Unveils," 2000).

THE ECONOMICS OF TIME SPENT ONLINE IN EUROPE
AFTER FREESERVE

Only 18 months after the launch of Freeserve, substantial consolidation was
predicted in the free ISP sector (Borzo, 1999; Chan, 1999; Doward, 2000).
Freeserve and other nontelecom free ISP players recognized early that survival in a highly competitive market would require a significant market share
plus revenue from advertising, online partnerships (with banks, retailers,
brokerage firms, travel businesses, and others), and electronic commerce
(Tomlinson, 1999). In short, businesses built along the lines of Freeserve
would have to become Internet portals offering content and services of value
(e.g., directory and search functions, notification services, e-mail, space for
personal Web pages, and direct links to sponsors). Fletcher Research predicted that the free ISP business model would largely disappear by 2002, as
firms like Freeserve and Altavista formed partnerships with dominant
telecoms (Godell, 2000). In 2001, Freeserve was acquired by France
Telecom's Wanadoo Internet service, but continued to operate under the
more recognizable Freeserve brand name.

Since the 1998 launch of Freeserve, the European Internet access market
has experienced tremendous change. Free ISPs encouraged millions to
adopt the Internet, demonstrating clearly that cost of access was a major deterrent to Internet growth in Europe. The free ISP phenomenon encouraged policymakers, interest groups, and the swelling ranks of Internet users
to bring pressure to bear on the most vexing cost deterrent to Internet
growth—the cost of metered dial-up access controlled by dominant
telecoms. This pressure and the need for the telecoms to remain competitive are achieving the desired outcomes, albeit slowly. Unmetered
narrowband access and limited broadband access emerged almost simultaneously throughout Europe, offering an array of choices to consumers and
a fragmented Internet access market (Godell, 2000).

The original free ISP business model, with its reliance on revenues from telephone connection charges, is hardly viable when alternative plans offer limited or unlimited unmetered access. Free Internet access combined with metered access would be attractive only to someone who ventures online seldom and for brief periods. For other low-income (or low-interest) Internet users, the less costly plans offering unmetered access during off-peak periods make more sense. Although such access services clearly support the policy objectives of regulators keen on extending the benefits of the Internet to all social strata, customers attracted by cheap access may not hold much interest for firms engaged in e-commerce and online media. Such firms will be far more likely to target consumers with the desire and ability to afford plans providing more online time or the full benefits of broadband. These access customers will have to decide between available unmetered narrowband access or broadband access at premium prices.

The ability of European Internet users to connect for longer online sessions has improved since the introduction of Freeserve and the other free ISPs. However, it is highly unlikely that the nations of Europe will ever experience the wide availability of unmetered narrowband access enjoyed by Internet users in the United States. The Internet access market will remain substantially stratified throughout most of the first decade of the new century. Without significant intervention from national or pan-European regulators, the former national telecoms will continue to control access tariffs in order to maximize their profits and subsidize both the cost and risk associated with a range of new technologies needed in all of their areas of operation. Time spent online by European consumers will continue to increase, but at rates that will continue to frustrate policymakers and slow the growth of Internet-based media and other online entrepreneurs.

Alternative access technologies like wireless and digital television introduce more options. At the same time, however, the enormous costs associated with providing both Internet access and compelling content worthy of the cost of broadband connections will drive consolidation in the Internet access market. The winners in the consolidation stakes are most likely to be the dominant telecoms. Like Freeserve, smaller ISPs and firms like chello are far more likely to be acquired for their customer bases than to succeed independently. Even AOL Europe faces a risky future without partnering with dominant telecoms. In the end, success in the Internet access market will depend on market share. It will be ironic if the competition and consumer choice fostered by the free ISP movement disappear with consolidation, especially if the former national monopoly telecoms regain near-total control of Internet access in Europe.

REFERENCES

220,000 French customers signed up for free Internet access. (1999, June 22). *Le Journal du Net*. Retrieved Nov. 21, 1999, from http://www.journaldunet.com/presse/englfree.shtml

27 Million Europeans will have broadband access by 2005, according to Forrester. (2000, August 1). *Forrester Research*. Retrieved August 24, 2000, from http://www.forrester.com/ER/Press/Release/0,1769,371,FF.html

Baker, S., Echikson, W., & Robinson, A. (2000, February 2). Europe's Internet bash. *Business Week* (3667): EB40–44. Retrieved April 10, 2000, from the online database Academic FullTEXT Elite [EBSCO Industries, Inc.].

Battle for the Internet. (2000a, March 7). *BBC News*. Retrieved April 8, 2000, from http://www.bbc.co.uk/hi/english/business/newsid_667000/667778.stm

Battle for the Internet. (2000b, August 22). *BBC News*. Retrieved September 13, 2000, from http://www.bbc.co.uk/hi/english/business/newsid_%5F667000/667778.stm

BBC fights back online. (1999, January 25). *Fletcher Research*. Retrieved November 29, 1999, from http://www.fletch.co.uk/about/content/press250199.html

Berendt, A. (1999, March). Carriers widened the net. *Telecommunications* (international ed.). Retrieved November 23, 1999, from http://www.telecoms-mag.com/issues/199903/tci/berendt.html

Borzo, J. (1999, December 13). A free ride. *The Wall Street Journal* (interactive ed.). Retrieved April 15, 2000, from http://www.wsj.com/archive/retrieved.cgi?id=944586441245545529.djm

Broadband blues. (2001, June 23). *The Economist*, (359), 8227, 62.

BT fears foreign takeover. (2000, February 18). *BBC News*. Retrieved April 8, 2000, from http://www.bbc.co.uk/hi/english/business/newsid_647000/647563.stm

BT offers unmetered net access. (1999, December 7). *BBC News*. Retrieved April 8, 2000, from http://www.bbc.co.uk/hi/english/business/newsid_554000/554072.stm

Cavallaro, M. (2001, February 16). Surfing, German style. *The Industry Standard*. Retrieved July 3, 2001, from /0,1902,22285,00.html

Chan, K. (1999, November 5). Freeserve CFO sees signs of consolidation in U.K. ISP mkt. *The Wall Street Journal* (interactive ed.; Dow Jones Newswires). Retrieved November 27, 1999, from http://www.wsj.com/archive/retrieve.cgi?id=DI-CO-19991105-002676.djml

chello broadband, n.v. (2000). *chello broadband, n.v. company info*. Retrieved April 22, 2000, from http://www.chello.com/company_info/P/751/index.html

chello unveils Europe's first study of broadband Internet usage. (2000, March 17). *Asia Pulse*. Retrieved April 27, 2000, from online database Academic FullTEXT Elite [EBSCO Industries, Inc.].

The cost of connecting. (2000, March 8). *BBC News*. Retrieved April 8, 2000, from http://www.bbc.co.uk/hi/english/in-depth/Internet price_wars/newsid 670000/670304.stm

Daniel, C., & Grande C. (2000, August 26). *Europe's fight for low-cost Internet access*. Retrieved August 30, 2000, from http://globalarchive.ft.com/globalarchive/article.html?id=000826000491

Datamonitor: Video and audio streaming traffic to increase. (1999, March 1). *Nua Internet Surveys*. Retrieved November 21, 1999, from http://www.nua.ie/surveys/?f=VS&art_id=905354735&rel=true

Doward, J. (2000, March 12). Unlimited access starts the real race to carve a cyberspace. *The Guardian* (Unlimited). Retrieved April 22, 2000, from http://www.guardianunlimited.co.uk/Archive/Article/0,4273,3973074,00.html

Durlacher Research Ltd. (2000). *The Durlacher quarterly Internet report* (Q4, 1999). London: Author.

eMarketer. (2001, April). *The broadband report*. New York: Author.

Essick, K. (1998, November 16). Running up the bill. *The Wall Street Journal* (interactive ed.). Retrieved April 15, 2000, from http://www.wsj.com/archive/retrieve.cgi?id=SB910920849350992500.djm

Essick, K. (1999, January 13). French netizens plan second Web boycott. *The Industry Standard*. Retrieved Nov. 21, 1999, from http://www.thestandard.com/article/display/0,1151,3129,00.html

EU drive for cheaper net access. (2000, April 4). *BBC News*. Retrieved April 8, 2000, from http://www.bbc.co.uk/hi/english/business/newsid_701000/701231.stm

Europe to remain in broadband slow lane. (2001, June 11). *Strategy Analytics*. Retrieved June 25, 2001, from http://www.strategyanalytics.com/press/PRDM028.htm

Flat-rate or unmetered access is critical for pervasive Internet economy. (1999, October 21). *International Data Corporation*. Retrieved April 21, 2000, from http://www.idc.com/Data/Europe/Content/EU102199PR.htm

France no longer lagging in Internet stakes. (2000, April 17). *Nua Internet Surveys*. Retrieved April 24, 2000, from http://www.nua.ie/surveys/?f=VS&art_id=905355722&rel=true

Freeserve unmetered move. (2000, March 14). *BBC News*. Retrieved April 8, 2000, from http://www.bbc.co.uk/hi/business/newsid_676000/676863.stm

Gatsoulis, J. (1999, October). Internet companies spin off free service to central Europe [Electronic version]. *Advertising Age International*, pp. 40–41. Retrieved November 19, 1999, from online database Academic FullTEXT Elite [EBSCO Industries, Inc.].

German household Internet use soaring. (2000, April 13). *Nua Internet Surveys*. Retrieved April 24, 2000, from http://www.nua.ie/surveys/?f=VS&art_id=905355717&rel=true

Godell, L. (2000, April 26). Europe's free Internet lunch fades away. *Fletcher Research Internet Newsletter, 3*(005), 2–3. [E-mail newsletter service]. London: Fletcher Research.

Goff, D. H. (1998). The United Kingdom. In A. B. Albarran & S. M. Chan-Olmsted (Eds.), *Global media economics: Commercialization, concentration and integration of world media markets* (pp. 99–118). Ames: Iowa State University Press.

Goff, D. H. (2000). Issues of Internet infrastructure. In A. B. Albarran & D. H. Goff (Eds.), *Understanding the web: Social, political, and economic dimensions of the Internet* (pp. 239–265). Ames: Iowa State University Press.

Grande, C. (2000, August 22). BT in flat-rate internet offer. Retrived August 30, 2000, from http://news.ft.com/ft/gx.cgi/ftc?pagename=View&c=Article&cid=FT3AQSLW7CC

Griffiths, D. (1999, June). Turning Internet into TV. *Telecommunications* (international ed.). Retrieved November 23, 1999, from http://www.telecoms-mag.com/issues/199906/tci/webtv.html

Harvey, F. (2000, August 22). Inching away from metered access. Retrieved August 30, 2000, from http://news.ft.com/ft/gx.cgi/ftc?pagename=View&c=Article&cid=FT3VLEHK7CC&live=true

Hilburn, M. (2001, March 23). Flat rate a fat bust in Europe.*Wired.com*. Retrieved June 26, 2001, from http://www.wired.com/news/print/0,1294,42556,00.html

How many online (Europe)? (2001). *Nua Internet Surveys*. Retrieved November 8, 2001, from http://www.nua.ie/surveys/how_many_online/europe.html

Kane, B. (1999, April 1). To pay or not to pay? *The Guardian* (Unlimited). Retrieved April 22, 2000, from http://www.guardianunlimited.co.uk/Archive/Article/0,4273,3847163,00.html

Malim, G. (1999, October). Competition has not delivered choice: Western Europe–United Kingdom. *Telecommunications* (international ed.). Retrieved November 23, 1999, from http://www/telecoms-mag.com/issues/199910/tci/uk.html

More than 10,000 new users try the Internet each day in Britain—survey findings. (1999, March). *NOP Research Group*. Retrieved January 24th, 2000, from http://www.nop.co.uk/survey/internet/internet_item2.htm

Moroney, J. (1999, July). Stalking the telco's Trojan horse. *Telecommunications* (international ed.). Retrieved November 23, 1999, from http://www/telecoms-mag.com/issues/199907/tci/digitv.html

Morrell, S. (2000, April 27). The effect of TV-based Internet access on customer service. *Datamonitor.* Retrieved April 27, 2000, from http://www.datamonitor.com/viewnewsstory.asp?id=410&pa=TC

Nairn, G. (1999, October 8). Fundamental changes to UK industry. *Financial Times* [FT Telecoms: Interactive Media: Internet]. Retrieved November 11, 1999, from http://www.ft.com/ftsurveys/sp662e.htm

Ni hEildhe, S. (1999a, February 1). Are European telecoms hindering Net growth?. *Nua Internet Surveys*. Retrieved November 21, 1999, from http://www.nua.surveys/analysis/weekly_editorial/archives/issue1no60.html

Ni hEildhe, S. (1999b, May 25). The net's Babylon. *Nua Internet Surveys*. Retrieved November 21, 1999, from http://www.nua.ie/surveys/analysis/weekly_editorial/archives/issue1no76.html

Nuttall, C. (1999, July 29). ADSL price tie for consumer. *BBC News*. Retrieved April 8, 2000, from http://www.bbc.uk/hi/sci/tech/newsid_406000/406819.stm

OECD. (2000, March 16). OECD Internet access price comparison. *Organization for Economic Co-operation and Development*. Retrieved April 15, 2000, from http://www.oecd.dsti/sti/it/cm/stats/isp-price99.htm

Oftel. (1999, November). *Pricing of calls to the Internet: Possible initiatives to bring about appropriate and flexible tariffs*. London: Office of Telecommunications.

Owens, S. (2001a, May 23). IDC predicts nearly 1 billion Internet users will fuel more than $5 trillion in Internet commerce by 2005. *IDC News*. [E-mail newsletter]. Available from http://www.idc.com

Owens, S. (2001b, June 18). Digital tv at the heart of convergence in the European communications market. *IDC News*. [E-mail newsletter]. Available from http://www.idc.com

Pringle, D. (2000, February 21). Clickable viewing. *The Wall Street Journal* (interactive ed.). Retrieved April 15, 2000, from http://www.wsj.com/archive/retrieve.cgi?id=SB948905708265366280.djm

Rohde, L. (1999, September 20). BBC throws hat into U.K.'s free ISP ring. *Infoworld, 21*(38), 40. Retrieved November 19, 1999, from online database Academic FullTEXT Elite [EBSCO Industries, Inc.].

Rudiez, A. (2000, February 25). ISP: Free market in search of revenue stream. *Connectis (Financial Times)*. Retrieved March 3, 2000, from http://www/ft.com/specials/sp730a.htm

Sharkhunt.com: Internet startup launches online revolution. (1999, July 15). *Financial Times*. Retrieved November 27, 1999, from http://www.globalarchive.ft.com/search/FTJSPController.htm

Simpson, D. (2000, February 10). AOL Europe offers Germany slice of "new economy." *Reuters* (Yahoo! News). Retrieved February 10, 2000, from http://dailynews.yahoo.com/h/nm/20000to10/wr/economy_aoleurope_1.html

Telcos and TV vie for digital tv market worth over $100 billion by 2005. (2000, December 14). *Ovum*. Retrieved June 30, 2001, from http://www.ovum.com/press/pressreleases/default.asp?wp=dtt.htm

Telecom titans dial M for mayhem. (1999, October 17). *The Guardian* (Unlimited). Retrieved April 22, 2000, from http://www.guardianlimited.co.uk/Archive/Article/0,4273,3913321,00.html

Telekom scraps T-Online flat-rate Internet access. (2001, February 15). *Handelsblatt*. Retrieved July 3, 2001, from http://www2.handelsblatt.com/hbiwwwangebot/fn/relhbi/sfn/cn_artikel_drucken_e/docid/384558/SH/0/depot/0/index.html

Tomlinson, R. (1999, September 6). Internet free Europe. *Fortune, 140*(5), 165–169. Retrieved November 11, 1999, from online database Academic FullTEXT Elite [EBSCO Industries, Inc.].

Tomorrow's Internet. (1999, November 13). *The Economist, 353*(8145), 23–25. Retrieved November 22, 1999, from online database Academic FullTEXT Elite [EBSCO Industries, Inc.].

Tony Blair's full speech. (2000, March 7). *The Guardian* (Unlimited). Retrieved April 22, 2000, from guardianunlimited.co.uk/Archive/Article/0,4273,3971304,00.html

Trager, L. (1999, May 26). Free net: It's a Euro thing. *Inter@ctive Week*. Retrieved November 23, 1999, from http://www.zdnet.com/filters/printerfriendly/0,6061,404635-35,00.html

U.K. ISP audience proves difficult to categorize. (1999, July 26). *Nua Internet Surveys*. Retrieved November 21, 1999, from http://www.nua.ie/surveys/?f=VS&art_id=905355056&rel=true

Williams, B. (2000, September 25). *Interconnect: Arthur Andersen's Weekly News Summary for the Technology, Media, and Communications Industries* [Online serial], *6*(37).

8

ADVERTISING AND INTERNET USAGE: A PERSPECTIVE FROM TIME AND MEDIA PLANNING[1]

Francisco Javier Pérez-Latre
Universidad de Navarra

In 1995, what appeared to be an urgent integration of cable television, computing and telephone technologies seemed to be able to completely modify the media landscape (Pérez-Latre, 1995). The announced—and even hyped—*convergence,* technically feasible, has not been possible yet from a commercial point of view. The most relevant development has taken place on the Internet, especially the World Wide Web and e-mail.

The Internet has experienced a unique evolution, different from the rest of the media because of its fast-growing pace, faster than the media that came before it. According to Internet analyst Meeker (1996), it took radio 38 years to reach 50 million homes, TV 13 years, and cable as an advertising and entertainment medium 10 years. In contrast, it has taken the Internet only 5 years to reach 50 million homes. Even though the rate of adoption of the Internet as a new communication tool has accelerated faster than any previous medium, the rate of adopting it as a new method of shopping ap-

---

[1]For questions contact: Dr. Francisco Javier Pérez Latre, Departamento de Empresa Informativa, Facultad de Comunicación, Universidad de Navarra, 31080 Pamplona (ES). Phone: +34 948 42 56 55; e-mail: fjperez@unav.es

pears to have lagged. Retail sales on the Internet represented only 2% of all U.S. retail sales in 1999.

Traditional retail stores have also been slow to adopt the Internet as a vital retail outlet. As late as February 1999, well-known retailers such as the Gap, Sears, and Bloomingdales were not among the top 25 web shopping sites in the country. Perhaps, the slow pace of consumers' and retailers' adoption of the Internet as a shopping outlet helps to explain why little published empirical research has focused on ordering merchandise on the Internet.

INTERNET USAGE AND ADVERTISING EXPENDITURES IN TELEVISION

At the beginning, the Internet looked like a natural competitor for television and print media. But, in a way analogous to what happened in the very beginning of cable television, the Internet has become a new mode of presenting television, radio, and print media—a distribution channel for new media content. It has also served to remarkably accelerate advertising spending in conventional media, at least until the dot.com stock slowdown that started in the spring of 2000.

Significantly, the effect of portals, search engines, and online media has been an increase of advertising expenditures in conventional media, especially television. The advertising of Internet-related brands was notably increased in the first half of 2000 in the United States. However, a change later occurred that could have impact in the future: Internet and World Wide Web brands reduced their advertising expenditure after the stock exchange decline. Space sellers in the Internet benefited from this new situation, as Internet brands put more emphasis in online advertising.

Internet advertising, including Internet-only brands and traditional companies online, accounted for 6.4% of all advertising in the first half of the year 2000. This category became the advertising sector with highest share in the overall advertising market. The increase was significant compared to the first half of 1999, when Internet advertising market share was just 1.8%.

In television, the market has some unique characteristics. Internet advertising cluttered television during 1999 and the first half of 2000, but decreased by June 2000. The category reached its highest market share at 8% in November 1999, in a period of intense expenditures marked by the Christmas season. That reality was apparent in the number of spots related to dot.com companies that were broadcast in the 2000 Super Bowl (arguably the most important advertising event in the year in the United States when a number of high-profile campaigns are rolled out). However, by June 2000, market share had decreased to 5.4%.

It was during the Super Bowl, in January 2000, when Internet brands reached their peak level of spending on network television. As much as 8.6% of total advertising expenditures on ABC, NBC, CBS, Fox, UPN, and WB came from Internet-related companies. By June, the figure had gone down to 6%. When Super Bowl 2001 came, trade magazines were positing questions about how advertising inventory was going to be sold by ABC/ESPN, the network in charge of the event. Out of 23 advertisers in the Super Bowl, just 3 were Internet-related brands (E-Trade, Hotjobs.com, and Monster.com), in sharp contrast with the year before. Conventional advertisers Federal Express, Anheuser-Busch, Frito-Lay, MasterCard, Philip Morris, Coca-Cola, Sony, Levi Strauss, Subway, Visa, Universal, and Warner Bros. dominated the advertising for the 2001 Super Bowl.

The changed landscape prompted *Advertising Age* to explain to their readers that "last year's prices were inflated by the dot-com frenzy, in which some seventeen dot.coms bought Super Bowl spots. At least one, Netpliance.com, paid a shocking $3 million-plus for its ad, according to executives—the most ever by a Super Bowl advertiser. Following the dot.com collapse, this year's bowl will get off almost dot.com free, with only Net vets E-Trade, Hotjobs and Monster.com making a return appearance" (*Advertising Age*, January 15, 2001, p. 42). It seems that Internet brands are trying to reduce advertising costs and thus are looking for advertising spaces more suited to their target audiences. Such brands show some degree of reluctance to mass advertise on the networks.

Cable television presents a different kind of picture. Advertising expenditures remained pretty stable after peaking in November 1999, when Internet brands amounted to as much as 12% of overall advertising expenditures for cable. However, from April to June 2000, the advertising share of the market in cable television went down to 10%. Obviously, cable television is a medium better suited to reach targeted audiences than is network television.

Building a consistent brand image is still a major goal to most dot.coms. In an environment of clutter with a large number of brands, advertising in cable networks seems to be a fair strategy. News channels such as MSNBC, CNN, and Fox News Channel and business and financial channels like CNNfn, CNBC, and Bloomberg are in a good position to broadcast advertising with potential for communicating with investors and Internet users who work in managerial settings.

Nevertheless, a trend to reduce Internet advertising expenditures appeared. On the 2001 Oscars Award ceremony, just one online ad campaign was shown (*Advertising Age*, March 19, 2001). A Merrill Lynch survey significantly played down previous expectations for Internet expenditures. In 2001, Merrill Lynch forecast a decline in online ad spending of 25%, to $6 billion (still a large figure) from an earlier estimate of $8 billion. Ads from dot.com companies comprised 65% of online ad spending in 1999. By 2001, the figure amounted to 20%. The first quarter in year 2001 was the worst. A modest rebound was expected for 2001's second half (*Advertising Age*, March 19, 2001).

THE DIGITAL DIVIDE

When share of advertising market is analyzed and an assessment is made about how many people are online in the world, a reality appears. It has been classified as "the digital divide" and is depicted in Table 8.1. By August 2001, 65% of the Internet population lived in the United States, Canada, and Europe. Latin America, Africa, and the Middle East lagged in Internet households with less than 6% of the Internet population. In 2001, Denmark had the highest proportion of households connected to the Internet at 54%, closely followed by the United States (50.9%). Singapore, Taiwan, and Korea took the remaining positions in the top five, with household penetration rates of 47.4%, 40%, and 37%, respectively (Net value, March 26, 2001. www.nua.net).

In a good part of the world, communication speed is still a scarce resource. Internet services tend to shape themselves initially as electronic information systems—new ways of providing media content to users. The Internet is a medium that challenges conventional rules and integrates sound, image, and text. It is also present in the rest of media, because it allows for frequent calls to their web pages.

In terms of demographics, the Internet attracts males with higher education and incomes. Women have been increasing online usage rapidly, as shown in Table 8.2. In the United States, women make up the majority of the Internet audience. In Canada there is a virtual tie in gender composition, with countries like Australia and Brazil, rapidly reaching similar levels. However, in the largest European countries, males remain a clear majority, with figures higher to 60% of the Internet universe.

Although sharing some elements of the overall European landscape, Spain provides a different framework for Internet audience analysis. In 2000, 7% of the Spanish population used the Internet. The general audience for the rest of the media is remarkably higher: for newspapers it is 35.2%; magazines, 53.3%; radio, 53%; television, 89.4%, and movies, 10.2%. Therefore, we should not exaggerate the influence of Internet, although its growth is remarkably fast. In 1996, only 1% of the Spanish audience reported using the Internet, increasing to 2.7% in 1997, 4.6% in 1998,

TABLE 8.1
Internet Users in Selected Global Regions (August, 2001)

Area	Internet Users	% Total Users
United States & Canada	180.68	35
Europe	154.63	30
Asia/Pacific	143.99	28
Latin America	25.33	5
Africa	4.15	.008
Middle East	4.65	.009
World total	513.41	100

Source: How Many Online? NUA Internet Surveys, www.nua.net.

TABLE 8.2
Percentage of Internet Users, by Gender, in Selected Countries (December 2000)

Country	Male	Female
United States	48.9	51.1
Canada	50.7	49.3
Australia	53.3	46.7
Brazil	57.3	42.7
Netherlands	60	40
Japan	60.2	39.8
United Kingdom	60.7	39.3
Germany	62.1	37.9
Italy	63.6	36.4
France	64.1	35.9

Source: Adapted from Advertising Age, March 5, 2001, p. 29.

and 12% by 2000 (Asociación para la Investigación de Medios de Comunicación, 2000). The media has almost doubled its audience every year. In the most densely populated urban areas, the amount of users is even higher, with 11.5% in Catalonia and 9.7% in Madrid.[2]

The sustained growth of personal computers among Spanish households is also remarkable. In 1999, the number of households connected to the Internet reached 27%. The Internet will continue to grow rapidly, reaching new sectors in Spanish society. The growth of Internet audiences have also had an immediate impact on advertising expenditures, which grew 600% between 1998 and 1999. Still, the Internet accounts for only 1.6% of total advertising expenditures in Spain (Lozano, 2000).

INTERNET ADVERTISERS

Internet advertisers are mostly companies directly related to hardware, software, and the Internet itself. The incorporation of other advertisers to the Internet is slower than expected. In the United States, dot.com companies continue to buy more online advertising than do traditional companies, and smaller companies buy more advertising than do large companies. Although

---

[2]In this case, Madrid refers not only to the capital but also to the overall Madrid region

large companies increased their online advertising in the fourth quarter of 2000, the average number of ad impressions purchased amounted to only 135 million impressions. The average number of impressions bought by small companies[3] topped 167 million, whereas the average number of impressions bought by mid-sized dot.coms reached 453 million.

Online ad placement shows a similar pattern in the United Kingdom. In 1999, there was a concentration of spending in computing and Internet-related brands, which made up 33% of overall advertising placement. Entertainment (23%), financial services (22%), and news and reference (22%) were also key sectors.

It should be remembered that the Internet is the first medium that emerged without advertiser sponsorship, which came later (Strangelove, 1994). At the beginning, the Internet was used to build and keep brand image. Every company seemed to need to be there, without thinking about the business model that could make Internet presence cost efficient. By and large, advertisers came to the Internet by imitation; they couldn't afford not to be present in this new medium.

According to eMarketer, almost 85% of U.S. advertising and marketing companies believe that the most important reason for using online advertising is to drive traffic to websites. Other reasons for using online ads include brand building, branding, and sponsorship opportunities. By the end of 2000, 77% of marketers and ad agency executives were planning to increase ad spending in online media, whereas only 5% intended to decrease their spending, in spite of slower economic conditions. The major obstacles preventing companies from increasing their spending on Internet ads included budget limitations, low click-through rates, and the high cost of ads (*eMarketer,* February 28, 2001. In www.nua.net).

The present challenge resides in commercial transactions. It seems obvious that the Internet will increase revenues (Grant, 1999). The most visited websites in the United States—the pioneer country in the Internet's development—are usually portals, as shown in Table 8.3.

It is interesting to realize that besides overall audience, time is a significant factor. Audiences grant to portals a degree of time that is not uniform. On average, people spend approximately 27 minutes at Yahoo, 19 minutes at Microsoft Corp., 17 minutes at AOL/Time Warner, and 7 minutes at Terra Lycos (*Advertising Age,* April 10, 2001). In portals more directly linked to commercial transactions, like eBay, audience time averages 47 minutes. If portals are ranked according to time spent, a different picture emerges, as shown in Table 8.4.

Among different countries, a mixed reality appears. In the countries with the largest active Internet universe, users already spend a significant amount of time online. However, there is still notable room for growth (as shown in Table 8.5), especially when time dedicated to other media is taken into account.

---

[3]Small companies are defined here as those with quarterly sales of under $75 million.

TABLE 8.3
Top 10 Visited Properties in the United States (February 2001)

Website	Unique Audience
AOL Time Warner	27,997,000
Microsoft Corp.	23,612,000
Yahoo!	21,353,000
Terra Lycos	6,736,000
Excite@Home	6,546,000
eBay	4,745,000
Walt Disney Internet Group	4,736,000
eUniverse Network	3,593,000
Amazon.com	3,454,000
About.com	3,414,000

Source: *Advertising Age*, February 12, 2001, p. 26.

TABLE 8.4
Average Time Spent in the 10 Most-Visited Websites in the United States
(February, 2001)

Website	Average time spent (minutes:seconds), by Adults Age 12 and Up
eBay	47:53
Yahoo!	27:16
Microsoft Corp.	19:07
AOL Time/Warner	17:07
Excite@Home	15:55
Walt Disney Internet Group	13:44
Amazon.com	8:53
eUniverse Network	7:41
Terra Lycos	7:23
About.com	6:11

Source: *Advertising Age*, February 12, 2001, p. 26.

TABLE 8.5

Average Online Time Spent per Month Among Top 10 Countries (December 2000)

Country	Average Time Spent per Month on the Internet (hours:minutes:seconds)
Canada	9:24:08
United States	8:41:36
Germany	8:15:54
Japan	7:41:36
Brazil	7:08:08
Netherlands	6:51:08
Australia	6:43:49
Italy	6:05:56
France	5:56:10
United Kingdom	5:24:56

Source: Advertising Age, March 5, 2001, p. 29.

Most Internet advertising spaces are known as *banners*, a peculiar kind of outdoor advertising applied to the Internet, complete with animation and more information access. Best-performing banners can reach 13.5% of the U.S. population (*Advertising Age*, February 12, 2001). The Internet is still a medium for small audiences. The percentage of banner ads that are clicked through is low—click rates are typically below 1%. The countries with the highest click rates are shown in Table 8.6.

Online newspapers are also part of the Internet. A comparison of audience versus time spent could also be made looking at the number of visitors in Spanish online newspapers and comparing it to the number of visited pages. It presents a different picture, as shown in Table 8.7.

The number of pages visited may be a good indicator of time spent with each website. The table indicates no direct correlation between the number of visitors and number of visited pages. Perhaps this reflects the dedication of audiences toward online newspapers. Sometimes dedication can be a useful variable that could overcome a lower number of visitors to a web page. More time in a particular website also allows advertisers more opportunities for readers to notice an ad.

The analysis of online newspapers in Spain reveals one trend: The business and financial press have an online presence that is proportionally higher than the strength of their paper editions in the overall press market.

TABLE 8.6
Percentage of Banner Ads Clicked Through in Selected Countries (December 2000)

Country	Click Rate
Ireland	0.82
Hong Kong	0.63
Germany	0.58
Spain	0.55
Denmark	0.52
Singapore	0.51
Netherlands	0.50
Japan	0.49
Sweden	0.49

Source: *Advertising Age*, March 5, 2001, p. 29.

TABLE 8.7
Daily Visits to Online Spanish Newspapers, and Average Pages by Visit (July 2000)

Online Newspaper	Daily Visits	Average Pages by Visit
El País Digital	108,103	7
Marca Digital	81,433	15
El Mundo	81,115	10
ABC	32,370	10
As Digital	23,682	4
Expansión Directo	15,181	20
Cinco Días	12,002	6
La Vanguardia Digital	12,235	10
El Periódico online	11,096	11

Source: www.ojd.es. *Oficina de Justificación de la Difusión* (Spanish Audit Bureau of Circulation), July 2000.

Such a situation makes sense, because a significant number of readers of financial and business press used computers to gain valuable insights on the economy and business before the Internet became a relevant medium. Expansión Directo, the online newspaper with the highest number of visited pages in the period studied, is a business and financial newspaper. One other daily in the category, Cinco Días, also fares well in comparison with its overall number of readers.

A NEW PARADIGM IN COMMUNICATION: BIDIRECTIONALITY AND USE OF TIME

The Internet brought a change in the paradigm for spreading messages and the capacity to interact with audiences, which has given hope to researchers, advertisers, and audiences alike. Internet users tend to be oriented to content. Their culture is oral; nothing impedes you to send a message. Spam and unsolicited advertising can lead to many complaints among Internet users.

Conventional media and commercial communication are notably unidirectional. They decide how we should be informed, educated, or entertained, with a limited ability to respond to t he audiences. On the other hand, internet users answer, react, and struggle to participate in message configuration. Probably this reality has also had an impact on conventional media like broadcasting and print, where a trend to foster audience participation is also apparent.

It is anticipated that a new media landscape produced by Internet development will be defined by a set of messages, texts, and images. The objective of this competition is readers' and viewers' time. Needless to say, time is not unlimited. One who dedicates more time to a medium will be dedicating less time to the rest. Audience growth with the Internet since 1996 coincides in time with a certain decline of newspaper audience and even the stabilization of television audience. In Spain, between 1996 and 2000, television lost 2 rating points after decades of continuous growth propelled by a certain liberalization of the market (first when commercial terrestrial television debuted, followed by the initial development of cable and digital platforms that broadcast via satellite).

A well-publicized study conducted by Nielsen and released by America Online in August 1998 reported that people with Internet access watched 15% less television than did those without Internet access. Typically, more educated and affluent people using the Internet tend to watch less television. Other studies, such as one released by Price Waterhouse in October 1998, contend that America Online is underestimating the damage that the Internet is inflicting on TV. Price Waterhouse suggested the Internet is eroding the TV audience by as much as 34% (Frankel, 1998).

Nieto expressed this idea quite lucidly several years ago: "The main consumption made by the consumer of information does not belong to the media company but to the consumer ... the consumption of his time ... the struggle to gain time is the most notable goal in the information market" (Nieto, 1990, p. 81).

Bogart expressed a similar idea: The public consumes the media much "in the same way that consumes some other products and services, paying for them not only whit money but also with their time" (Bogart, 1994, p. 11). The present situation looks perplexing and uncertain. Globally, media consumption has increased, but less time is dedicated to each medium. At the same time, one medium does not substitute for another: they adapt and readapt, as history has taught us. For example, in Spain, all conventional media except cinema had higher global audiences in 1999 than in 1980 (AIMC, 2000).

Worburg (1999) called attention to the scarce research that advertising has devoted to time. It should be noted that Worburg's research focuses on television and not the Internet, but some of its conclusions can still be applied here. Television facilitates time ratings because it imposes on the viewer its own rhythm of advertising and programming. These tactics will not work with print media and the Internet, because users' control and freedom to choose is higher. Time, as Worburg said, is "finite merchandise" (Worburg, 1999, p. 419). It could well be stated that time, even though it may have connotations that reflect commercial use, is more than just merchandise.

On the other hand, Internet advertising poses new challenges. The audience is attracted to very specific information and, being active, tends to avoid advertising. Advertisers understand this new reality and are becoming suspicious of Internet advertising, which in this stage of development is mirroring the advertising practices of conventional media by using banners. Even though banners are to some extent interactive, they resemble conventional print media or outdoor advertising spaces. New problems of advertising measurement are found. The audience of the Internet is not, by any means, the audience of advertising on the Internet.

The public decides about the kind of Internet content it considers interesting, of value, and trustworthy. The era of captive audiences—of distinct and recognizable advertising time slots in to which the audience was pushed while watching a program or waiting for it—seems to have come to a close with the Internet. The public has, at the very least, a new ability to choose.

This also explains why major advertisers are reluctant to invest in high Internet advertising expenditures. They tend not to be content with banners alone but also require click-through rates in those banners, a deeper indication of audience involvement with advertising messages and higher potential for recall. Advertisers know that most banners are a hassle for the audience and are passed by accordingly. Still, the Internet is here to stay: "The mainstreaming of the Internet is inevitable, but it will not happen easily" (Ephron, 2000, p. 52).

The consequences of Internet development for advertising media planning are slowly becoming apparent. Nielsen has published a study called

Multi Media Mentor. The study tries to provide a level playing field of measurement for five media: television, radio, newspapers, magazines, and the Internet. People over age 12 spend an hour of a day on the Internet in the United States, which is hardly a surprising finding.

However, direct comparison to other media is worth mentioning. The Internet gets 12% of media consumption time—double that of newspapers (5%) and three times that of magazines (4%). Time spent with media is shifting to more time spent online. Cable television provided a good lesson. At its start, cable attempted to tie its share of dollars to its share of television viewing, arguing that advertisers had to follow the consumer. What began in 1981 as a proposal that advertisers put 5% of their television dollars into cable has grown to 30% by 2000 (Ephron, 2000). The time spent by U.S. audiences on the Internet suggests that national advertisers may underutilize the medium.

Ephron argued that the main obstacle to Internet advertising media planning evolution has been the branding approach utilized to advertise in the Internet:

> The Internet preempted branding—an old agency buzzword—in an attempt to escape trial by click-through. Web sellers used branding to focus advertisers on the value of banners that is not captured by measuring click-throughs. This includes creating awareness, improving brand imagery and increasing purchase intent. But "branding" was an unfortunate choice, because agencies think that banners, with their limited message, can not be used for branding. … A priori, long-message [media] such as television print and radio are better able to brand than are short-message media, such as out-of-home, point-of-purchase and the Internet. The Internet is not for branding. Reminding makes more sense. (Ephron, 2000, p. 52)

CONCLUSION

The variety of options in the communications arena has provoked a situation in which it is difficult for one to stand out, point up, or be original, which seems to be the goal in a very competitive field. The capacity to adapt to changes that occur at a faster pace each day is going to become a true competitive asset (Law, 1994).

Therefore, it is important not to lose sight of the background environment that seems key in advertising media planning and utilization of the Internet. What is more crucial is the decision-making process. This challenge of being original may become dangerous if the more dramatic and spectacular configurations prevail in a landscape of message inflation. If the intent of advertisers resides only in provoking interest, then the Internet has its limitations.

Media and education are at a crossroads. New technologies widen our intellectual horizons and also grant rapid access to powerful information resources. But the computers of the digital and interactive revolution do not think. They cannot be substitutes for personal decision making. Philips put it eloquently: "[It] is impressive. Is magic. The possibilities are infinite. And, nevertheless, if is not usable to his own master—the adequate idea—it will suddenly become something terribly boring. It simply strikes our attention, but then we feel disappointed" (Philips, 1994, p. 30). The attraction that the new media provokes shouldn't make us forget the primacy of ideas—the "grey matter" that is the very core of communication activities.

The conclusion that may be extracted from the diffusion of the Internet and new media development has dimensions of hope, but also concern. The new technologies offer technologies for freedom, with new opportunities for public participation and free discussion. But quite often this leads to the prevalence of data without analysis, the concentration of information sources, or the incapacity to present information in its historic context and manipulation. Nieto got to the core issue underlining content quality: "Technological innovations provide easy access to more information in less time. However, it is not so important to reach more people in a shorter period of time than to satisfy their information needs in an adequate way" (Nieto, 2000, p. 11).

The new technologies of communications offer new forms of making us reflect or preventing us to think, to obstruct reflection or make it easier. And that confirms once again the secondary value of technical aspects in communication, and the key consideration deserved by advertising content.

It is not so relevant through which medium we are having a dialogue; what is important is what we are saying. It is crucial for communication to promote dialogue, peace, coexistence, and human dignity. The Internet, in this regard, offers fresh and interesting possibilities, especially for advertising.

REFERENCES

Asociación para la investigación de medios de comunicación [AIMC]. (2000). *Marco general de medios en España 2000.* Madrid: Author.

Bogart, L. (1994, March–April). Who pays for the media? *Journal of Advertising Research,* pp. 11–18.

Ephron, E. (2000, November 13). Net generating anxiety as it rewrites the rules. *Advertising Age,* p. 52.

Frankel, D. (1998, November 12). The Net vs. the tube. *E! Online News.* Retrieved from http://tv.eonline.com/News

Grant, I. (1999, July/August). Branding sites are dead, long live e-commerce. *Admap,* pp. 39–41.

Law, A. (1994, January). How to wave the ride of change: Advertising and agency are now outdated concepts. *Admap,* p. 29.

Lozano, I. (2000). La publicidad.com cambia el sector. *Dinero, 828,* 36–38.

Meeker, M. (1996). *The Internet report.* New York: Harper Business.

Nieto, A. (1990). Marketing e información. *Comunicación y Sociedad, 3,* 67–84.

Nieto, A. (2000). *Time and the information market. The Case of Spain.* Pamplona: Eunsa.

Pérez-Latre, F. J. (1995). Publicidad y nuevos medios. *Comunicación y Sociedad, 8,* 133–141.

Philips, R. (1994, March 31). Remember the idea. *Campaign,* pp. 30–31.

Strangelove, M. (1994). *How to advertise on the Internet.* Ottawa: Strangelove Internet Enterprises.

Worburg, J. M. (1999). Time: The "silent" cultural value in America television. *Journalism & Mass Communication Quarterly, 76,* 419–432.

9

MEDIA MARKETS AS TIME MARKETS: THE CASE OF SPAIN[1]

Alfonso Nieto
University of Navarra

INTRODUCTION

Time is one of the few things that we all possess (Seneca, 1982). We are all granted 24-hour days, 7-day weeks, 12-month years. But one question haunts us: How much time do we really have? It is difficult to define something so common and universal and, at the same time, so uncertain. Saint Augustine's perplexity persists in our time. "What, then, is time? If no one ask of me, I know; if I wish to explain to him who asks, I know not" (St. Augustine, 1995, p. 14).

Humans are temporary beings; they live in time, not as owners, but rather as possessors; they can use it, enjoy it, take advantage of it, waste it, but never recover it (Polo, 1993). Humans spend time and, when they use it, they make a time investment for eternity.

Only as a metaphor can it be said that humans "produce" time, inasmuch as they configure it and fill it with work to produce goods or provide services. Today's transcendental conception of time responds to the free exercise of human work, which manages to surmount its own temporality,

[1]For questions, contact: Dr. Alfonso Nieto, Departamento de Empresa Informativa, Universidad de Navarra, 31080 Pamplona (ES). Phone: +34 948 425655; e-mail: anieto@unav.es

because working much and well is altogether meaningful if it is the gateway to eternity (Elchardus, 1991).

Being possessors of time—not owners—entails use and application, but also external conditions that are the result of the free exercise of liberties. The abundance and the scarcity of time are related to the ability to be critical, the capacity to accept or reject information; in short, the ability to exercise personal responsibility. The consequence of those conditions is the paradox of time, inexplicable for many citizens. As the time of a life span increases, time spent working decreases, but people live with the sensation of being pressured by the shortage of time (Comisión Europea, 1997). People experience the anxiety of time as they think more about the swiftness of its flight than about the tranquility of the moment. This anxiety associated with time becomes particularly evident in the information market, in which the escalating potential consumption of information products and services clashes head on with the inexorable finiteness of people's time.

TIME IN THE INFORMATION MARKET

The information market can be defined as the physical seat or the social sphere where the supply and the demand for information products or services come together (Nieto & Iglesias, 1993). The advances of information and communication technology are expanding the scope of this market (e.g., the home, or a given social group) with areas of tastes and practices difficult to demarcate until now (sports, hobbies, professional specializations, etc.). The information market is increasingly a content market that aims to satisfy the needs of specific audiences (Nieto, 1996).

One of the central components of the information market is time, an essential element in both supply–demand relationships and mediation activities. To consume information products is to consume time, an intangible, immaterial commodity, although it can be quantitatively measured and qualitatively valued. Contrary to the consumption of time that also occurs with other products and services (the price of which is independent of time in most cases), in the information market the value of the content is intimately related to the amount of people's time that it is capable of attracting. The time market finds one of its natural headquarters in the information market. This is so largely because one of the most important functions of time in the information market is to make it possible to go from ignorance to knowledge, the transit from not knowing to knowing. At one point, there is ignorance and, at another, there is knowledge. The passage from one to another state supposes consumption of time during a specific time span.

Time and information have a common note in their origin: They are both intangible, immaterial realities. This condition makes it difficult to conceive the union of both terms—time information—without prejudice to it being increasingly present in individual and social life, to offer goods and services, provide entertainment, accelerate economic and financial processes, and so on. Time is an essential present reality in the whole information process (Cousido, 1989) and in each of the elements that participate in the stages of carrying out that process: materialization, industrialization, and commercialization (Nieto, 1996).

The subjects of the information relationship (reporter, mediator, receiver), the tasks involved in developing the message to situate it on the appropriate support, the multiplication so that the content can get to numerous receivers, and the necessary marketing for a proper economic exploitation—all these need time, spend time, and employ time. In information, time directly affects the organized structure (e.g., company, organization) and the activity of disseminating printed, audiovisual, electronic, and other forms of media. Time has a legal and economic projection in the information enterprise in addition to the informative aspect. It drives information changes in addition to witnessing them; it is present in all the messages and in all the media (Cousido, 1989). In addition, time in itself is an object of information. The fact that some media (print, electronic) differentiate their distinct supports, schedules, or services precisely by their temporal nature has a lot to do with the centrality of time in the information market.

In summary, information time is the duration, total or partial, necessary for a product or service of that nature to be produced, disseminated, or consumed in the information market. Understood in this way, information time is the object of supply and demand in the market. To illustrate this reality, we focus our attention on the supply side of this market, by analyzing the time attention that different media attract in one specific market, that of Spain.

TIME SUPPLY IN THE INFORMATION MARKET: THE CASE OF SPAIN

The time supply for consuming information will be effective if it finds a positive response among those demanding time for the product that it has put into circulation. The demand will be successful if it achieves acceptance among those willing to supply time. Time demand and product supply on one hand, and product demand and time supply on the other, are two relationships that intertwine, irrespective of their free or burdensome nature. In fact, in the information market, those demanding products or services may or may not pay, but what is always present in the exchange relationship is the supply and demand of time.

When the receiver of information products relinquishes time, he or she becomes part of the audience, which can be considered as an aggregate of people's time. The time/audience ratio is a common measurement in the information market. It admits a variety of assessments depending on the condition and quantity of time and audiences. Circumstances unrelated to the information market can alter this ratio. An example is the increasing time devoted to work in the service sector, which already takes up more than 60% of the total employment in the European Union (Comisión Europea, 1997), or the current tendency to replace the analysis of working time during the week with approaches having an annual or biannual framework (Du Roy, Freys, & Meyer, 1990).

The audience/time ratio requires a third element to participate in multi-national, national, or local markets: the medium that is the object of supply and demand of information time, traditionally classified according to the form used for dissemination (e.g., press, radio, television). The label "new media" includes some mediums derived from earlier ones as a consequence of innovations in communication and information technologies.

Next we try to illustrate this new way of seeing the information market from the perspective of time, explicit by studying the effective supply of time for the various mass media among the Spanish population. The analyses that follow are grounded on the interrelationships among the three elements already mentioned: audience, medium, and time. They try to show the varied structures of time devoted to the different media in the different autonomous communities in Spain.

The time unit adopted here is the minute, applied to the three modes of supplying and demanding time: reading, listening, and viewing. As to the period studied, the analysis focuses primarily on the second half of the 1990s, with more detailed data on the year 1997. I have used the fundamental sources that study Spanish information markets with regularity, including the following: (a) Instituto Nacional de Estadística (INE—National Statistics Institute); (b) Asociación para la Investigación de Medios de Comunicación (AIMC—Association for Mass Media Research), which produces (c) the Estudio General de Medios (EGM—General Media Study), the principal survey on media consumption in Spain.

Population and Audiences in Spain: Basic Data

The information market involves the interaction of people that supply and demand time for consuming information products and services. The people that participate in the market respond to a variety of social, economic, and geographical situations. They form groups of varying sizes. The study of time requires considering some basic data that facilitate subsequent analyses. The tables that follow summarize two groups of data referring to the Spanish market: population, and audiences and time. Table 9.1 reflects the distribution of the Spanish population by gender and age (14 and older).

The home is the base of the information market in that it configures a specific type of consumer sphere that can be called the *information home* (Portilla, 1998). It is the physical and environmental location where most people in Spain receive and consume information services and products.

Table 9.2 lists households by autonomous community (AC), specifying the percentage corresponding to each as well as the average number of people in the household. Four autonomous communities (Andalusia, Catalonia, Community of Valencia and Madrid) account for 56.29% of all

TABLE 9.1
Population, by Gender and Age (14 and older)

Age	Population	(%)	Total Men	(%)	Total Women	(%)
Total	33,984,501	100.0	16,618,422	48.9	17,366,080	51.1
14–19	4,180,093	12.3	2,141,024	6.3	2,039,070	6.0
20–24	3,670,326	10.8	1,869,148	5.5	1,801,179	5.3
25–34	6,864,869	20.2	3,466,419	10.2	3,398,450	10.0
35–44	5,607,443	16.5	2,820,714	8.3	2,786,729	8.2
45–54	4,350,016	12.8	2,175,008	6.4	2,175,008	6.4
55–64	3,806,264	11.2	1,835,163	5.4	1,971,101	5.8
65+	5,505,489	16.2	2,310,946	6.8	3,194,543	9.4

Source: INE and AIMC (1998).

Spanish households. Adding Castile-Leon, Galicia and Basque Country (País Vasco) to these four accounts for 75.03% of Spanish homes. There are no large differences in the average number of people in each household, which, nevertheless, varies between the maximum of 3.28 people in the Canary Islands and the minimum of 2.64 in the Balearic Islands. Nine ACs fall below the average (2.87). These data are pertinent to subsequent analyses of audience/household and time/household ratios.

These basic data about population structure by ages and by household type illustrate the diversity of the regions in the Spanish market. This diversity also appears, perhaps more extremely, when considering the population in generic terms as an effective media audience.

Basic Audience/Time Data.   *Audience* refers to the set of people that, at a given point in time and in specific markets, accept information products or services. The audience configures a market with its time supply. The penetration of a product (program, copy of a newspaper or a magazine, etc.) is directly related to the time that each market (in this case, each autonomous community), considered globally, offers into circulation.

Table 9.3 provides a general view of the audience across different types of media. It displays the percentage of the Spanish population (14 and older) that regularly consumes each type of medium. This table shows, on one hand, the growth of the number of people over 13. Over the time period examined there is a general decrease in audience usage across all the media, except dailies and cinema. In some cases, the loss has been progressive for years; for example, supplements have been losing audience since

TABLE 9.2
Spanish Households, by Autonomous Communities

Autonomous Community	Households	(%)	Average Number of People in Household
Andalucía	1,966.746	16.60	3.03
Aragón	397,004	3.34	2.67
Asturias	356,370	3.00	2.68
Baleares	246,279	2.09	2.64
Canarias	436,993	3.70	3.28
Cantabria	155,277	1.30	2.95
Castile-La Mancha	509,877	4.30	2.72
Castilla-León	801,579	6.76	2.73
Cataluña	1,947,949	16.43	2.76
Community of Valenciana	1,212,884	10.23	2.83
Extremadura	317,557	2.70	2.76
Galicia	788,532	6.65	2.98
La Rioja	84,727	0.71	2.77
Madrid	1,545,630	13.03	2.89
Murcia	297,913	2.51	3.02
Navarra	156,501	1.32	2.93
País Vasco	633,027	5.33	2.89
Spain (total)	11,854,845	100.00	2.87

Source: INE (1998).

1994, whereas magazines have not recovered the percentage achieved in 1992. Television maintains greater stability, but radio goes up and down. In general, the data of Table 9.3 suggest a change in the overall and relative attention captured by the various media.

TABLE 9.3
Percentage of Media Usage in Spain Among People Aged 14 and Older
(1992–2000)

Year	Universe	Dailies	Supplements	Magazines	Radio	TV	Cinema
1992	32,000	33.6	36.6	57.9	52.4	89.5	6.9
1993	32,000	36.4	37.9	56.2	52.9	90.1	7.6
1994	32,332	36.8	36.1	54.0	55.4	90.4	7.8
1995	33,576	38.0	33.8	54.7	56.5	91.1	8.3
1996	33,794	38.2	32.9	55.6	56.6	91.3	9.3
1997	33,984	37.2	32.4	54.7	55.0	90.7	8.8
1998	34,132	36.9	31.9	53.2	53.5	89.2	10.2
1999	34,497	35.2	31.3	53.3	53.0	89.4	10.2
2000	34,733	36.3	32.1	53.6	52.9	89.2	11.0

Source: AIMC (2001).

Table 9.4 provides the overall data corresponding to 2000, broken down by autonomous communities. Although they are not used later, the data referring to the Internet are included to round out this general view of media usage in Spain. The situations are varied and the penetration of the media in the different autonomous communities provides contrasts worth noting. For example, in the daily press, Navarra ranks first with a penetration of 60.2%, three times that of Castile-La Mancha, in the last position with 19.6%.

These differences in media penetration by geographic area and by medium are also evident when media consumption is analyzed. Table 9.5 summarizes the evolution of the consumption of time by media between 1997 and 2000. During this period, the average time for media consumption per day was around 6 hours per capita, but its distribution and intensity by media and regions were quite different. The data in Table 9.6 refers to the average daily time consumption, expressed in minutes, that each of the autonomous communities devoted to the various sectors on an average per person. Three media sectors are selected for comparison: daily press, radio, television. Table 9.6 reveals noteworthy differences in the time devoted to three media. The difference of time spent reading dailies between Navarra (22 minutes) and Castile-La Mancha (8 minutes) is particularly striking. In radio, 37 minutes separate Murcia's maximum and the minimum of the Balearic Islands. Also significant is the difference of 74 minutes in the time devoted to television between Castile-La Mancha and Asturias.

This generic study of audiences and average per capita time consumption by autonomous community and media must be completed with the

TABLE 9.4

Media Penetration, by Audience in autonomous regions (2000) (%)

Regions	Dailies	Supplements	Magazines	Radio	TV	Cinema	Internet
Andalucía	27.4	21.3	48.7	50.3	91.2	9.9	10.1
Aragón	40.4	40.8	54.6	52.2	88.5	9.9	12.2
Asturias	51.5	48.3	61.1	62.1	88	8.4	10.7
Baleares	49.2	33	65.7	48.8	86.4	15.1	13.7
Community of Valenciana	32.4	29.8	57.2	49.4	89.9	11.1	12.5
Canarias	39.2	16.2	52.8	51.3	86	11.5	11.7
Cantabria	58.6	56.8	67.2	55.8	90.8	7.8	9.3
Castile-La Mancha	19.6	14.3	44.9	43.7	91	8.4	8.3
Castilla-León	39.5	32.8	54.2	53.9	89.5	10.4	8.8
Cataluña	39.5	36.1	60.7	54.9	89.8	13.6	18.6
Extremadura	28.5	19.2	50.2	46.8	93.9	9.7	6.9
Galicia	37.6	34.8	42.4	48.5	87.1	6.7	8.2
La Rioja	40.5	48.4	55.1	59.7	92.9	10.5	17.3
Madrid	32.3	34.2	51.4	56.9	86.9	13.2	16.3
Murcia	30	29.3	52	54.6	87.7	10.8	8
Navarra	60.2	46.9	54.1	57.4	91.2	9.2	13.8
País Vasco	58.4	60.2	59.1	61.1	87.5	12	14
Spain (total)	36.3	32.1	53.6	52.9	89.2	11	12.6

Source: AIMC (2001).

TABLE 9.5
Media Consumption: Daily Average Time (minutes) per Capita (1997–2000)

	1997	1998	1999	2000
Dailies	15.0	14.7	14.2	15.2
Supplements	2.0	2.2	2.0	2.3
Magazines	5.7	4.8	4.5	4.6
Radio	100.0	96.0	95.0	95.0
Television	231.0	222.0	224.0	222.0
Internet				5.5
Total	359.4	344.4	344.2	349.1

Source: AIMC (2001).

specific analysis of the peculiarities of the time offerings for reading, listening, and viewing.

Time for Reading

Reading requires an effort to grasp the meaning locked in the written text; it is a way of discovering knowledge. Because the languages used for communicating through the printed word are different, knowing how to read in various languages places one in an advantageous position for acquiring varied knowledge. The various kinds of knowledge imply different readings and different readers, depending on age, mental situations, tastes, and occupation.

How much time is spent reading print media? Table 9.7 displays data that can be the basis for finding a first answer. For that purpose, the AIMC 1997 Methodology Report defines reading time as the distribution of readers according to the reading time that they declare. The mean is calculated for the following segment categories: less than 15 minutes (average 7.5 minutes), from 15 to 30 minutes (average 22.5 minutes), from 30 to 60 minutes (average 45 minutes), and from 60 to 120 minutes (average 90 minutes). The second column of Table 9.7 lists, in thousands, the number of media titles circulating in Spain. The figure results from taking a reading done on a given title as a base, that is, a person can make various readings in various print media.[2]

---

[2]The 1997 AIMC Methodology Report defines average readings per copy as the number of reading occasions per copy. The calculation is made with the number of different times the publication has been read during the last publication period. As to the term *Readings,* an individual's contact with a given publication in a given period is called a *reading.* As a result, the number of readings takes into consideration the fact that one individual may have read more than one publication.

TABLE 9.6
Daily Media Consumption, in minutes, by Autonomous Communities (1997)

	Dailies	Radio	TV	Total
Andalucía	11	95	248	354
Aragón	14	100	233	347
Asturias	18	111	190	319
Baleares	18	82	209	309
Canarias	14	93	208	315
Cantarina	21	96	249	366
Castile La Mancha	8	85	264	357
Castilla-León	15	101	204	320
Cataluña	16	114	254	384
Cxommunity Valenciana	13	105	253	371
Extremadura	11	85	256	352
Galicia	13	85	197	295
La Rioja	18	113	222	353
Madrid	13	96	216	325
Murcia	11	119	224	354
Navarra	22	103	198	323
País Vasco	21	111	200	332
Average/total	14	100	2ɔ1	345

Source: AIMC (1998).

TABLE 9.7
Reading Time in Print Media in Spain (1997)*

	Readings	Average Time (minutes)	Readers	Average per reader	Average per capita	Daily Average percapita
Dailies	18,167	27	12,815	38	14	14
Supplements	16,148	37	11,018	54	18	3
Weeklies	21,737	42	11,834	77	27	4

*Figures in thousands, time in minutes.
Source: AIMC (1998).

The column headed with the title "Readers" indicates, in thousands, the total number of persons who read each type of printed medium. This figure is a result of applying the percentage of average audience to the total universe or potential audience. For example, 37.7% is the average percentage of penetration in dailies, which, in reference to the universe of 33,982,000 people, gives us 12,815,000 readers. The average time of the fourth column results from relating the first and second columns with the third. The per capita time and the per capita/day averages are the consequence of applying the initial data to the various categories: 365 days, 52 weeks, 26 weeks, 12 months.

From Table 9.7, we conclude that press readers use printed publications around an hour a day. About 38.2 minutes are offered to the daily press. The per capita/day average of the potential reader population is around 23 minutes.

An interesting aspect for better understanding this market is the geographical distribution of the time supply. Table 9.8 breaks down the per capita/day times for three types of print media: dailies, supplements, and weekly magazines. The figures correspond to autonomous communities and the data is from 1997. Taken together, the supply is 21 minutes per capita/day. Listing the ACs from larger to smaller offerings provides a first approximation to the supply levels for attending to daily press consumption. The difference among the autonomous communities with greater and lesser time supplies is 19 minutes a day.

Time for Listening

Listening consumes time, and sometimes patience as well. Listening time is of particular importance to radio companies. This mass medium almost exclusively uses voice, both spoken language and music, to satisfy the needs of those who offer listening time (Conde, 1997).

Voices and noise, sound and words fill the waking hours that the citizen devotes—or that are pilfered from him or her—to listening. Noise abounds, sound is scarce, and silence barely exists. In fact, the absence of noise feels strange, a way of ignoring the value of silence.

Listening to the radio can be done from the most wide-ranging places and at the most varied times. According to Conde, radio configures various types of time: *historical time,* which transpires in current events and are expressed by the news radio; *cyclic time,* subject to the natural cycles of days, weeks, and so on; *institutional time,* the result of the legal ordering of time for study, rest, and travel; *biographic* or *generational time,* corresponding to a variety of ages with different tastes and interests; *personal time,* reflecting individual situations, states of mind, tastes, and so on; and *specific radio-listening time,* or time for the *I* with the radio, influenced by the other times (Conde, 1997).

Times that are looking at collective interests (historical, cyclic, institutional times) predominate on conventional (e.g., talk) radio, whereas times

TABLE 9.8
Average Audience (%) and Daily Reading Time per Capita,
by Autonomous Communities (1997)

	Dailie Audience	Average Time (minutes)	Supplements Audience	Average Time (minutes)	Weeklies Audience	Average time (minutes)
Andalucía	28.7	10.7	17.4	1.6	47.6	3.5
Aragón	38.6	14.3	41.3	3.8	54.6	4.0
Asturias	49.2	18.3	36.8	3.4	62.8	4.6
Baleares	47.3	17.6	36.0	3.3	65.7	4.8
Canarias	37.5	13.9	27.9	2.6	60.1	4.4
Cantarina	56.5	21.0	16.1	1.5	60.9	4.5
Castile-La Mancha	21.6	8.0	56.7	5.3	42.3	3.1
Castilla-León	41.1	15.3	20.3	1.9	52.9	3.9
Cataluña	43.5	16.2	35.2	3.3	61.6	4.5
Community Valencia	36.1	13.4	40.4	3.7	61.2	4.5
Extremadura	30.8	11.4	19.4	1.8	42.9	3.1
Galicia	36.3	13.5	29.3	2.7	43.4	3.2
La Rioja	48.7	18.1	42.2	3.9	49.1	3.6
Madrid	34.3	12.7	38.1	3.5	56.6	4.1
Murcia	28.6	10.6	26.0	2.4	52.9	3.9
Navarra	60.6	22.5	60.7	5.6	53.7	3.9
País Vasco	57.4	21.3	61.1	5.7	60.4	4.4

Source: AIMC (1998).

that respond to individual tastes (biographic and personal times) dominate formula (e.g., music) radio (Conde, 1997). The time for interacting with the listener will be determined by the point at which there is a match "between the listener's inner time and the time of the scheduling itself, a coupling, a connecting of the mentioned times" (Conde, 1997, p. 105).

That matching of supply and demand time for listening determines the audience levels of radio in general and of each type of station or broadcast in particular: amplitude modulation (AM), frequency modulation (FM); conventional radio (CR), or formula radio (FR). Table 9.9 displays the percentage

TABLE 9.9
Percentage of Radio Listening Audience in Spain (1992–2000)

Year	Total	AM	FM	CR	FR
1992	52.4	16.5	39.4	35.7	21.1
1993	52.9	18.2	38.5	37.3	19.9
1994	55.4	18.0	41.1	36.1	24.8
1995	56.5	17.9	42.3	38.7	23.7
1996	56.6	16.5	43.2	36.5	24.3
1997	55.0	14.9	42.7	34.2	24.4
1998	53.5	12.8	42.6	32.2	24.6
1999	53.0	11.2	43.3	31.0	24.7
2000	52.9	10.7	43.6	30.8	24.6

Source: AIMC (2001).

of the audiences in Spain from 1992 to 1997. The total radio audience[3] increased from 1992 to 1996. In 1997, radio audiences began to decline.

Taking 1997 as a reference year, the average penetration was 55.0% of the Spanish population over 13, which equals 18,715,502 people. The average time offered by listeners is 100 minutes a day. Both audience and time listening to radio are distributed differently among the autonomous communities. Table 9.10 specifies the details of the percentage of average audience in each of the autonomous communities, population corresponding to each, number of listeners, average daily offering of each listener in minutes, and the resulting total time in minutes. Nine autonomous communities[4] have audiences larger than 55%, which is the national average, and eight[5] have lower percentages. The largest time offerings are in Murcia, Catalonia, Basque Country, Asturias, and the Community of Valencia. The smallest time offerings are in the Balearic Islands, Castile-La Mancha, Extremadura, Galicia, and the Canary Islands.

---

[3]We assume the definition of average daily audience and minutes of listening adopted by AIMC in the 1997 Methodology Report. *Average audience*: Average number of individuals (expressed in absolute terms or as a percentage of the universe) that have listened to a given station throughout the specified period. The calculation weights each listener according to that listener's listening time. The arithmetic mean of the listeners can be obtained for each of the half-hours that make up the period analyzed. This indicator expressed in percentage (rating) is equivalent to the percentage that the per capita consumption amounts to for the total duration of the time interval considered. *Minutes of listening*: In relation to a station and a specific period, it expresses the average consumption per individual. This consumption can be per capita (referring to the total population) or per listener (restricted to the part of the population that has

[4]Aragon, Asturias, the Canary Islands, Cantabria, Castile-Leon, Catalonia, La Rioja, Navarre, and Basque Country.

TABLE 9.10
Radio Audiences and Time for Listening, by Autonomous Communities (1997)

	Audience (%)	Population	Listeners	Listening (minutes)	Total (hours)
Andalucía	53.2	5,965,841	3,173,827	95.0	5,025,226,7
Aragón	57.7	1,059,559	611,366	100.0	1,018,942,6
Asturias	63.5	955,179	606,539	111.0	1,122,096,5
Baleares	46.2	650,640	300,596	82.0	410,814,1
Canarias	56.5	1,410,419	796,887	93.0	1,235,174,4
Cantarina	56.5	458,618	259,119	96.0	414,590,7
Castile-La Mancha	42.6	1,384,397	589,753	85.0	835,483,6
Castilla-León	56.3	2,185,805	1,230,608	101.0	2,071,523,8
Cataluña	59.1	5,372,961	3,175,420	114.0	6,033,297,9

Source: AIMC (1998).

Time for Viewing

It is estimated that European citizens devote or supply between a third and half of the leisure hours that they spend at home watching television (Du Roy et al., 1990). This it is one of the most frequent activities in Spanish homes (CIRES, 1997). Nevertheless, a slow decline in television viewing is underway. An increasing number of people would like to reduce the time they spend watching television (CIRES, 1997).

In Spain, there are two acknowledged sources for studying audiences: the AIMC analyses mentioned above, and the Sofres Audiencia de Medios (Sofres Media Audience) that uses a panel of audimeters. Among other obvious methodological differences, one deserves highlighting. The AIMC universe consists of the population over the age of 13, whereas Sofres adopts a universe that starts at the age of 3.[6] For consistency of method and statistics, this study uses the data from the AIMC study. Table 9.11 displays the penetration of the televi-

---

[6]For example, in 1996 Sofres' universe, in thousands, was 36,600 people; for AIMC, it was 33,794.

TABLE 9.11
Television Audiences and Viewers (1992–2000)

Year	Population (thousands)	Audience (%)	Viewers (thousands)
1992	32,000	89.5	28,640
1993	32,000	90.1	28,832
1994	32,332	90.4	29,228
1995	33,576	91.1	30,588
1996	33,794	91.3	30,854
1997	33,984	90.7	30,823

Source: AIMC (1998).

sion audience in Spain from 1992 to 1997.[7] From a universe of 33,984,501 people, 90.7% of the 1997 audience makes a theoretical total of 30,823,942 viewers. The fact that the program with the largest audience in 1997 reached 11,775,000 people can give us an idea of audience accumulation.

For the first time in the history of television in Spain, the audience decreased in 1997, albeit by only a small number (31,000 viewers). The audience percentage dropped 0.60 points. Given that the population had increased by 190,000 people, the decline is proportionally greater. These data take on greater relevance when it is observed that from 1995 to 1996, the universe of population increased by 218,000 people and the number of viewers also rose by 266,000. As Table 9.12 shows, the television audience varies significantly depending on the autonomous community, in both people and the amount of time offered. The audience/time relationships are based on the average of 231 minutes a day devoted to television in 1997. In seven autonomous communities, the average of minutes is greater than the national average;[8] in ten, it is lower[9] and represents 44.4% of the audience. These seven regions with time offerings above 231 minutes account for

---

[7]We assume the definition of average daily audience and minutes of viewing adopted by AIMC in the 1997 Methodology Report. *Average audience*: Average number of individuals (expressed in absolute terms or as a percentage of the universe) that have seen a given station throughout the specified period. The calculation weights each viewer for his or her viewing time. The arithmetic mean of the viewers can be obtained for each of the half-hours that make up the period analyzed. This indicator expressed in percentage (rating) is equivalent to the percentage that the consumption amounts to for the total duration of the time interval considered. *Minutes of viewing*: In relation to a station and a specific period, it expresses the average consumption per individual. This average covers the total population.

[8]Andalusia, Aragon, Cantabria, Castile-La Mancha, Catalonia, Community of Valencia, and Extremadura.

[9]Asturias, the Balearic Islands, the Canary Islands, Castile-Leon, Galicia, La Rioja, Madrid, Murcia, Navarre, and Basque Country.

TABLE 9.12
Television Audience and Daily Time Viewing, by Autonomous Communities

	Audience (%)	Population	Viewers	Viewing (minutes)	Total (hours)
Andalucía	91.7	5,965,841	5,470,676	248	22,612,127
Aragón	90.5	1,059,559	958,901	233	3,723,732
Asturias	88.8	955,179	848,199	190	2,685,964
Baleares	90	650,640	585,576	209	2,039,756
Canarias	89.5	1,410,419	1,262,325	208	4,376,060
Cantabria	92.7	458,618	425,139	249	1,764,327
Castile-La Mancha	93	1,384,397	1,287,489	264	5,664,952
Castilla-León	89	2,185,805	1,945,366	204	6,614,244
Cataluña	92.6	5,372,961	4,975,362	254	21,062,366
Community of Valenciana	93.2	3,427,996	3,194,892	253	13,471,795
Extremadura	92.3	875,002	807,627	256	3,445,875
Galicia	88.5	2,347,716	2,077,729	197	6,821,877
La Rioja	96.4	234,335	225,899	222	835,826
Madrid	87.1	4,465,967	3,889,857	216	14,003,485
Murcia	90.8	898,801	816,111	224	3,046,814
Navarra	87	458,669	399,042	198	1,316,839
País Vasco	89.8	1,832,596	1,645,671	200	5,485,570

Source: AIMC (1998).

55.5% of the audience and offer an average of 251 minutes a day. The reading of the figures in the last column, with the total minutes per day that people that reside in the various autonomous communities supply, leads us to ponder the importance of time devoted to television and makes it possible to formulate considerations about possible alternatives for the use or employment of almost 119 million hours a day.

CONCLUSIONS

The consideration of media markets as time markets lends special attention to time supply and demand for reading, listening, and viewing contents. With time as a currency of exchange, the different media compete by attracting the attention of people, but more and more they also compete in retaining that attention as much as possible. In this sense, traditional reading, listening, and viewing of print or broadcasting content must be complemented by intensity of use. Audience shares and average time of consumption are the two essential variables that shape the aggregate supply of time. This is a supply essentially limited by the living conditions of people, their habits, occupations, physiological needs, age, income, and other variables.

Regarding the demand of time by the media, such limitations do not exist. At least in theory, a single media outlet with 24 hours of programming (in the case of broadcasting) or a few printed products are able to demand all the time available of people. Only one TV channel, in a hypothetical monopolistic market, could concentrate the attention of all time supply from that market. Of course, the majority of media markets are not monopolistic, but very competitive. In this situation, in which a limited resource is demanded by an almost limitless and increasing supply of content, analyzing how this limited resource is allocated in aggregate terms seems crucial.

The objective of this chapter has been to investigate the aggregate structure of time supply for media consumption in the Spanish market. On one hand, the data illustrate the main changes in media audience shares between 1992 and 2000. Using 1997 as a reference point, we have analyzed the key figures on average time of daily media consumption. In order to show the remarkable variety of market situations across a national market, the supply diversity of time differs among geographic regions. This variable of analysis, used only as an example, is one that can be used in future studies to classify different markets defined by the configuration of their media time offerings.

This study comes up with some interesting conclusions, although more thorough research is needed. In spite of increasing content supply experimented with in Spain during the 1990s, audience shares and the time spent with media did not vary significantly; it was just redistributed.

Second, audience penetration and time consumed for different media show very significant differences by geographic regions. Although some of those differences can be correlated with such factors as income (e.g., newspaper reading), others do not seem to have a clear explanation.

When understood as a limited resource, time to read, listen, and watch can be subject to analysis, in addition to traditional investigations on individual media time budgets. New longitudinal research on the evolution of time supply for different media, as well as studies on the variables that influence the temporary structure of consumption of different markets, in aggregate terms, can offer new light on the consideration of media markets as markets of time.

REFERENCES

Asociación para la investigación de medios de comunicación [AIMC]. (1997). *Informe Metodológico de la AIMC [AIMC methological report]*. Madrid: Author.

Asociación para la investigación de medios de comunicación [AIMC]. (1998). *Marco General de los Medios en España 1998 [Media in Spain: General framework (1998)]*. Madrid: Author.

Asociación para la investigación de medios de comunicación [AIMC]. (2001). *Marco General de los Medios en España 2001 [Media in Spain: General framework (2001)]*. Madrid: Author.

CIRES. (1997). *La realidad social en España [Social reality in Spain]*. Bilbao: Fundación BBV, Fundación Bilbao Bizkaia Kutxa, Fundación Caja Madrid.

Comisión Europea. (1997). *La construcción de la sociedad Eeuropea de la información [The building of the European information society]*. Luxemburgo: Oficina de Publicaciones de las Comunidades Europeas.

Conde, F. (1997). Tiempos de radio [Radio times]. *II Encuentro Internacional AIMC sobre investigación de medios*. Madrid: AIMC.

Cousido, P. (1989). Manifestaciones temporales de la información [The temporal dimensions of information]. *Documentación de las Ciencias de la Información, 12*, 113–145.

Du Roy, O., Freys, J. C., & Meyer, A. V. (1990). *Hacia una política general del tiempo [Toward a general policy of time]*. Dublin: Ed. Fundación Europea.

Elchardus, M. (1991). Rationality and the specialization of meaning. A sociological approach to the allocation of time. In G. Antonides, W. Arts, & W. F. Van Raaij (Eds.), *The consumption of time and the timing of consumption. Contributions in honor of Amitai Etzioni* (pp. 69–86). Amsterdam: Koninklijke NederlandeAkademie.

Instituto Nacional de Estadistica [INE]. (1998). *Encuesta de Presupuestos Familiares*. Madrid.

Nieto, A. (1996). Tendencias en la configuración de la empresa informativa [Trends in the configuration of information companies]. *Derecho privado y constitución, 10*, 183–208.

Nieto, A., & Iglesias, F. (1993). *Empresa informativa [Information company]*. Barcelona: Ariel.

Polo, L. (1993). *Quién es el hombre. Un espíritu en el mundo [Who is the human being? A spirit into the world]* (2nd ed.). Madrid: Ediciones Rialp.

Portilla, I. (1998). *Consumo de televisión y hogar en España. Análisis estadístico. [Household structure and TV consumption in Spain]*. Unpublished doctoral dissertation, Universidad de Navarra, Pamplona, Spain.

Saint Augustine. (1995). *Confessions*. Oxford, UK: Oxford University Press.

Séneca, L.A. (1982). *Cartas a Lucilio [Letters to Lucilio]*. Barcelona: Juventud.

10

TRADING TIME AND MONEY FOR INFORMATION IN THE TELEVISION ADVERTISING MARKET: STRATEGIES AND CONSEQUENCES [1]

Patricia F. Phalen
The George Washington University

INTRODUCTION

This chapter focuses on the role of time in the operation of U.S. electronic media markets by analyzing the information system that supports economic transactions.[2] It considers market participants' investment of time in gathering information prior to a media buy, and the use of that information in estimating the value of media time purchased.

Coase (1937) observed that information processing is a cost to using the market. As in any marketplace, trade in the market for advertising time depends on the availability and acquisition of relevant data (Phalen, 1996,

---

[1] An earlier version of this paper was presented at the International Media Management and Economics Conference University of Navarra, Pamplona, Spain, May 4–5, 2000. For questions, contact: Patricia F. Phalen, Assistant Professor, School of Media and Public Affairs, Electronic Media Program, The George Washington University, 805 21st St., NW, Washington, DC 20052. Phone: (202) 994-4016; Fax: (202) 994-5806; e-mail: phalen@gwu.edu
[2] What Stinchcombe (1990, p. 74) called the "information collection and processing apparatus."

1998). Trading partners invest a great deal of time in obtaining information, because without it the uncertainties of exchange render decision making arbitrary at best. However, in the real world of economic transactions, every exchange involves some element of uncertainty. Not only is information differentially available to market participants, but the information that is obtainable may be inadequate or simply wrong. Knowing this, rational economic agents will attempt to compensate for the deficiency by making price adjustments and developing institutional mechanisms (some formal and some informal) to guard exchange relationships (Phalen, 1996). Ultimately, market participants must balance the investment of their resources with the quality of attainable information. They will, for example, continue to invest time in gathering information until the point at which the added economic benefit of new or better information begins to decline relative to the perceived return on time invested in an alternative task.

The role of information in market exchange is often overlooked in economic studies of the advertising marketplace, usually because analysts assume that information is uniformly available. Theorists from various academic disciplines including economics (e.g., Williamson), sociology (e.g., Granovetter, Stinchcombe), and anthropology (e.g., Geertz) have challenged this assumption, emphasizing the importance of information flows in economic decision making. This chapter argues that information plays a central role in the market for broadcast advertising time by affecting the ways market participants understand their options.

There are several ways to incorporate information into an analysis of media markets. One way is to operationalize "quality," and study the effect of higher-quality information on the price paid for advertising time. This is the approach taken by Fournier and Martin (1983) and Webster and Phalen (1997), who defined quality as statistical reliability and hypothesized that better information (i.e., data that is close to correct most of the time) increases the prices demanded by sellers. Another approach—the one taken here—is to focus on the characteristics of information available in the marketplace, and identify compensatory strategies used by market participants. For example, they develop standard business practices that either compensate for low-quality information or provide access to better information. These coping mechanisms affect the economic organization of the market (Williamson, 1985).

This discussion of the media information system is supported by data gathered from interviews with buyers, sellers, and researchers in the advertising market.[3] Quotes from market participants are used to illustrate the flow of information in the marketplace, the potential obstacles to the acquisition and interpretation of data, coping strategies in the face of time limitations and informational deficiencies, characteristics of various types of information, and potential threats to trade.

---

[3]In total, 57 interviews were conducted (see Phalen, 1996). The subset of interviews referenced in this chapter are labeled A–R, and each includes a short description of the speaker's occupation.

THE INFORMATION SYSTEM

A logical starting point for understanding a market information system is to identify the knowledge that market participants must acquire to transact business. In the market for advertising time, they need data that will assist them in projecting audiences, and they need to keep track of prices and market conditions. The sources of information they use to address these uncertainties are varied ... and flawed. Professionals consult published sources such as syndicated audience research reports, trade periodicals, and industry trend reports. They also gain information by taking advantage of professional networks—talking to trading partners and competitors.

These two information sources, published data and professional networks, are reviewed in this section. But first it is important to note that "facts" do not constitute the entire information system. Socioeconomic analyses must consider the interaction of data with the people who interpret and use them—the individuals who form the basic information processing mechanisms of modern social organizations (Stinchcombe, 1990). These individuals filter information. They make choices about which information to gather, process, and disseminate to others, and their search for information is limited by time. Individuals have varying capabilities and backgrounds as well as complicated motives for their actions. They form a complex part of the information system that supports economic exchange (Phalen, 1996).

The advertising market relies on a system of information that is built on the expertise of professionals who know how to use it (see Phalen, 1996). The information system not only addresses the needs of the market, but in many ways it actually structures those needs by influencing the perception of a problem (Stinchcombe, 1990). For example, the ratings define what is "good," so programmers strive to improve audience ratings as their measure of success. Thus, decision making is predicated on the institutionalized information system, even though the information may actually address different needs—some better, some worse than others.

Published Information: Audiences and Market Conditions

Contrary to popular usage of the term, the product that advertisers buy is not simply the "time" that media institutions sell. Rather, it is the potential audience reached through a given commercial time slot. Two variables related to time affect the value of the advertising spot: time of day and duration of the commercial. Different dayparts are likely to attract different viewers; and the length of a spot affects its potential impact on them. But many other factors also contribute to the probability of reaching a desired audience.

The economics of mass media are driven by the measurement and estimation of audiences. For television, radio, and the Internet, these audiences are approximated by the ratings system administered by companies like Nielsen Media Research, Arbitron, and Media Metrix—to the point where the ratings themselves have become synonymous with "audience." The behavior-based measurements used by these firms are just one indication of the consumer and commodity models of audience that drive the industry (see Webster & Phalen, 1994).

Media outlets do not generate ratings for their own audiences. Rather, they rely on firms like Nielson to collect and process viewing data. This arrangement is a direct response to an information problem in the marketplace. Because viewers cannot be seen and counted, information about them is estimated using statistical techniques. These estimates must be provided by a firm that is independent of the media organizations, or they lose all credibility. Buyers are not likely to believe numbers generated by a programmer, for example, because the station or network has the incentive to inflate viewership to enhance the value of its product in the market. Betsy Frank, a senior vice president at Saatchi & Saatchi, summed up this situation as follows: "Certainly this [ratings being produced by the companies that would sell off them] will make people question whether the interpretation of the numbers is self serving ..." (Jensen, 1994, p. B13). A third-party ratings provider lends credibility to audience measurement because, at least in theory, it has no incentive to favor one client over another as long as all are paying for the measurement service. Even if the media can influence Nielsen methodologies, no individual station or network should have an advantage over its competitors in trying to influence the ratings.

Third-party provision of audience ratings also ensures more consistency and comparability. If individual media outlets provided their own ratings, every programmer would have the incentive to design a research system that would yield the highest ratings. Evaluation of audience estimates would involve learning each of the different methodologies and assessing their strengths and weaknesses, which would make the information demands of time buying unsustainable. Buyers need to make fast comparisons among media options (e.g., network television and syndication), as well as among competitors in the same service (e.g., ABC and NBC television affiliates in the same market). Even though methodologies sometimes change at audience measurement firms, a track record is established for programs and channels over time. This track record is built on the same type of measurement year after year, and this allows buyers to evaluate historical audience trends.

The slow growth of the local cable advertising market is often cited as an example of what happens when consistent and comparable information is unavailable in a market. At first, each cable network commissioned its own ratings from Nielsen, and these reports were only available to the network that paid for the information. Buying cable meant using several reports, each of which had to be interpreted differently. The buy was complicated, and most planners and buyers were unsure of how to go about it. One researcher on the time-buying side of the business put it this way: "Cable drastically underestimated the buyers' need for simplicity" (Interview A: ad agency media department—research). A researcher on the sales side agreed: "… Buyers usually tend to prefer the path of least resistance. So, the simpler the buy, the more they like it" (Interview B: syndication—research). It was not until Nielsen began producing consistent reports for cable that the cable ad buying process became more manageable.

Ratings are often referred to as the "common currency" in the electronic media advertising market. They provide a way to map viewer or listener characteristics—a mutually accepted means of knowing the audience. Deficiencies associated with audience ratings can be traced to structural threats to information quality, problems of definition and measurement, and the information-processing limitations of individuals.

Structural threats to information quality exist because both sides of the exchange relationship are vulnerable to the problem of holdup. Nielsen makes an investment in a research apparatus to measure audiences, and that investment cannot be deployed for other uses if the media discontinue their support. On the other hand, the media are vulnerable because the ratings firm controls the information they need to conduct business. Once the commitment to supporting the ratings system has been made, alternatives to that system are effectively denied (e.g., the SMART system in the United States), and the ratings firm might compromise the quality of the research product. Although the threat of harm to both parties under this structure is very real, trading partners decrease potential economic harm through the use of contracts (see Phalen, 1996).

Although ratings are collected by a third-party provider, the media and the ratings firms are not completely independent of each other. Media sellers take great interest in the reputation of the ratings product because it is in their best interests to maintain a credible audience measurement system. They monitor Nielsen procedures to ensure that the methods are reliable. They do this through their own research departments and through an industry organization called the Media Rating Council (MRC), which audits research methodologies on behalf of all its members. The media also monitor trading partners and competitors to "protect the integrity of whatever Nielsen's got out there" (Interview C: TV production/distribution—research). These monitoring activities serve a dual purpose. First, they help maintain a system that will be credible to advertisers and their agencies; second, they discourage competitors from trying to gain an unfair advantage through manipulation of the audience measurement process.

Definition and measurement are constant sources of debate in the industry. For example, buyers and sellers of advertising time often complain about the size and representativeness of samples. And, although they claim that statistics like standard error have little effect on business, buyers tend to compensate for lower-quality information. One way they do this is to reduce the price they are willing to pay. A research director offered this example:

Now smart people who are buying—people who's job it is to value ratings … they are going to be smart enough over time to account for some of the vagueness in the numbers. For instance, if there is a late-night TV show that had a household rating which is based on meters—which just measures whether the set is on and tuned to the station or not—and let's say it does a 2 or a 1. And then the demographics, which are based on diaries, ...show nothing. The [research] guy is going to go, "Yeah, late night. Set's on, it's getting a rating but nobody says they watched it—what does that mean? They fell asleep with the TV on." They won't completely say that's a bogus rating, but they will be a little more suspicious of it. They'll look at that a little more carefully. They will value it a little less. And that's where CPMs come into play and where valuing the price of a rating is much more subjective. And that's why you see values for certain shows with exactly the same ratings a lot higher than others. (Interview D: TV production/distribution—research)

This example refers to local market ratings, but agency buyers also report paying less for national options, such as syndication.

Because the audiences are less predictable, buyers also adjust their buying practices to account for uncertainties in ratings information. For example, they reduce the effect of error in small ratings by adding together audiences from many spots on the lesser-rated media options. Similarly, they insist on audience guarantees to reduce the risk inherent in buying on the basis of predictions.

Regardless of measurement problems, most market participants accept the ratings system as "given." This tacit acceptance of the system was evident in many of the interviews with industry researchers and salespeople. One summed it up as: "everybody is using the same racing form, right or wrong" (Interview E: ad agency media department—buyer/planner). Another noted, "The industry is reactive, conservative, entrenched with respect to audience" (Interview A: ad agency media department—research). The common sentiment was that the system works for the needs of buyers and sellers, so there is no real motivation for changing it. Researchers commented on the state of the industry as follows:

Whether you like it or not, the system has been in place for 40 years and it works. (Interview F: TV production/distribution—research)

As long as everybody accepts the rules and the game gets played, why change it? ... It's a business that plays out over the course of a year, and if the studio and the network and the advertising agency and the advertiser all agree to the same rules ... in the long run it all sort of averages out. (Interview D: TV production/distribution—research)

Buyers and sellers in the market for television audiences recognize that the current ratings system is not necessarily the "best" one in terms of information quality, but they argue that it provides other kinds of advantages, such as stability in the market. One researcher referred to this when he talked about AGB's unsuccessful attempt to compete with Nielsen in the U.S. market: "Not to say that AGB's numbers were or were not accurate. Even if they were accurate—even if they were proven to be more accurate than the Nielsen numbers, there was such a business built up on the Nielsen numbers and the ways of doing business...whole structures. This whole department and dozens like it" (Interview D: TV production/distribution—research).

The institutionalization of the current information system means that market participants, although they recognize problems with the data, are unlikely to seek substantive changes because the investment of time and money would outweigh potential benefits. Professionals spend many years developing information-processing skills that are specific to the system that already exists, and they pass along those skills to the people they train. The analytical system is self-perpetuating. As a research director noted:

> This is a business built on the status quo. We don't like change. And once there is a system in place, that's the system. And there are a lot of people who have been in jobs for long, long periods of time and unless there is a major turnover, a major change in the way of thinking, it's always going to be that way. As a researcher, I love the fact that there is only one [research] company. I just have to focus on Nielsen and I know everything that Nielsen does and what they produce and we have systems set up to get that information out. And it's great. The last thing I want right now is another ratings service coming in because that means that all my people would have to do twice the work. And the same amount of people with twice the work—who needs it? (Interview C: TV production/distribution—research)

Although the problems with the ratings may be glossed over during day-to-day negotiations, users frequently complain that Nielsen and Arbitron are monopoly providers:

> I think there is a concern about the quality simply because it is the only game in town. I think that Coca-Cola is a better company because Pepsi came along. I think that Hertz is a better company because Avis came along. And it is just competition that drives these things. I think that the studios—their competition has given us, we've risen to new heights. But—the logic says that the quality probably isn't as strong as it should be because there are no marketplace forces. (Interview F: TV production/distribution—research)

But the industry is faced with a paradox of information: two systems measuring an audience correctly should provide information that is very similar, if not identical (see Phalen, 1996). The real value of competition is that it motivates ratings firms to improve their product and/or lower the prices they charge subscribers. The threat gives media some leverage to require methodological improvements and better service. It is unlikely, however, that competing firms will provide a product like audience ratings over the long term. The cost savings in quality would not compensate for the cost of funding two parallel services. This opinion was echoed by two research professionals:

> If you are a company starting out, you can't expect people to give up a service that they already have and know and [for which they] have track records for something that is only supplying top-level things. ... By the time they get up

and running and actually produce enough years of data to get the bugs worked out and to get some trend data, and you have to do it all because you can't have people buying just network television, you have to have the cable data and you have to have the syndication data. Because agencies need all of that and they need it off the same database for the most part. And with each year it gets harder and harder to do it all because Nielsen, of course, has had a lot of time to develop this, and they can keep folding things in and improving whereas somebody new has to come out with all of it. It is difficult. (Interview G: syndication—research)

Part of the problem with any new rating system is that we have this huge monster of a business that is all built on operating in the Nielsen world. (Interview D: TV production/distribution—research)

This means that the television industry is unlikely to support a competing ratings firm after the required changes are made to the incumbent's methodology.

Even with only one provider, the potential for data collection on audience size, demographics, and buying habits is virtually unlimited. The volume and complexity of data to be processed can be overwhelming: "That is probably the biggest problem we have in this industry ... information overload. There are too many numbers coming from too many sources that are manipulated in too many ways" (Interview C: TV Production/Distribution—Research).

Market participants address this problem by rationalizing the decision-making process through routinization (Phalen, 1996; Stinchcombe, 1990). While this strategy standardizes (and thus facilitates) information choices, it can lead to an overreliance on mechanistic ways of processing data. As one market participant noted: "Things are so computerized, and the mentality is so 'you have to have every blank filled in.' ... And ... the computer systems are such that you have to have every demographic filled in ... even if it isn't something that applies to the [television] program" (Interview G: syndication—research).

While these streamlining efforts address time constraints and other limitations on individuals as information processors, they can also compromise the quality of the information system. As Loveridge (1993) noted, the heuristic devices employed by the actors to make complex and variable flows of information more manageable actually constrain the perceived range of choices. Over time, these options become tacitly accepted as "the way things are done."

Audience size and composition are not the only uncertainties in the market for advertising time. Buyers and sellers also have to keep up with market conditions and pricing, and they must do so in a rapidly changing environment. Several published sources are available to help them do this. Trade publications, such as *Broadcasting and Cable, Advertising Age,* and *Electronic Media* provide one source of information. However, the interpretation of this data is not always straightforward. Two people can read the same article and glean very different information, depending on their expertise in reading market signals. Experienced professionals know that the content of these trade publications often reflects self-interested revelations or opinions on the part of the industry participants whom journalists interview for their stories. It is, as one market participant noted, "a little bit of negotiation that takes place in the press" (Interview H: ad agency media department—management).

Independent consultants and industry analysts also publish market reports that are useful to buyers and sellers. For example, Paul Kagan Associates and Ephron, Papazian & Ephron, Inc. provide data about growth trends in the industry and the financial status of media companies. Robert Coen at McCann-Erickson provides analyses of industry economic trends, and organizations like Forrester Research publish reports that cover most aspects of the media business. Industry professionals cite these sources frequently.

The main function of these sources is to provide data about the market, but it is clear that they also have an influence on it. For example, sellers might use this information to help determine the CPM increases[4] that they can expect in the next buying season. In other words, the forecasts and assessments do not merely passively report what is happening; they influence decision making. A cable executive illustrated this:

> We listen to people like Coen who say 'the market will be up by 4%.' Then [people in the sales planning department] make their budget predictions based on that analysis. The budget that they set, in turn, helps to determine the prices that they charge. (Interview I: national cable network—ad sales)

Market participants draw on historical records to make pricing decisions. Prices in the national market are generally based on historical CPMs plus some factor adjustment that accounts for economic conditions. This means that buyers need to know what they paid for national time last year in order to judge a fair market price for next year. Agencies maintain detailed historical records that give buyers this information for each client.

Another useful source of pricing information is the material published by trade associations. The Syndicated Network Television Association, for example, calculates average costs for barter syndication and makes that information available to the industry. The prices are quoted by daypart, not by program, so the information can really only serve as a general guideline. Both the Television Bureau of Advertising (TVB) and the Cable Advertising Bureau (CAB) provide similar information for their members.

Standard Rate and Data Service (SRDS) also provides pricing information. It publishes data on rate card prices for individual broadcast stations. SRDS used to be a key source of pricing information in the industry, but that is no longer the case. Broadcasters seldom sell according to rate card, and the negotiated price varies considerably among customers. For the most

---

[4]CPM is the abbreviation for "cost per thousand" households or viewers.

part, market participants use SRDS to find information on audiences and personnel, rather than on rates. However, the source does give an indication of the magnitude of pricing differences among stations.

There are several other published sources of pricing data. Nielsen does a CPM study of networks that is used by cable, broadcast, and syndication. There is also an industry source called Competitive Media Reports (CMR),[5] which estimates the price of schedules in national and local markets. This organization monitors advertising placement and collects pricing information. They do this by talking to buyers and sellers and generating averages for specific programs or dayparts. In general, these estimates are used as a guide—buyers and sellers have no real incentive to tell the truth, so the numbers are imprecise estimates of the actual prices paid. One sales executive explained: "[A person collecting data at CMR] doesn't see contracts—doesn't know the real rates and doesn't know the ins and outs of each contract. Sometimes they can be pretty accurate, and [they] may have gotten better over the years" (Interview J: local broadcast—ad sales). He gave an example of a spot that was sold on his station. He saw it reported in CMR at $38,000, but he had the $30,000 contract for that spot on his desk. He also cited a problem with spots that are sold as broad rotators. These are spots that run at the discretion of the station or network, within certain wide parameters specified in the buy. Advertisers pay less for these spots than they do for spots that are guaranteed to run in high-audience time periods. A rotator might happen to fall in prime time, but it would only cost a fraction of the amount another prime time advertiser paid for guaranteed placement. CMR might assess this as a "prime time" spot, and therefore overstate the price in its reports.

As noted earlier, market participants who give information to organizations like CMR have the incentive to distort it. As one cable executive explained: "You are not going to give your average price. Someone who paid above average can get the report. And they say, 'I paid a 10 dollar CPM and you are telling me you are selling it for 8—I overpaid.' So everyone tends to give their highest price" (Interview K: national cable network—ad sales). But even with this limitation, there is a general sense in the market that the numbers reported in CMR are a fair indication of the magnitude of differences and the direction of pricing trends. As the same salesperson put it, "You probably lie consistently" (Interview K: national cable network—ad sales). As is the case with audience ratings, market participants accept deficient information if the expenditure of money or time to gain higher-quality data exceeds its potential contribution to lowering the cost of advertising time or improving the efficiency of a buy.

Spot Quotations and Data (SQAD) offers another source of product pricing information. This company monitors prices in individual television markets, and issues summary reports. The information is used by planners at agencies to allocate media budgets. Nielsen's MonitorPlus uses SQAD in-

---

[5]Formerly the Broadcast Advertiser Reports (BAR).

formation to estimate the advertising expenditures in TV markets, serving the same function on the local level that CMR provides on the national level.

Buyers and sellers watch competitive strategies very closely. As one salesperson noted, "I have to know how many dollars are in the marketplace, and how many I want to go after" (Interview L: local broadcast—ad sales). Sources such as CMR and MonitorPlus give salespeople an efficient way to learn about advertiser strategies, because they record which firms are spending money in specific media. It would be impossible for each individual seller to monitor all broadcasts and compile this information. Networks, syndicators, and stations use the data to target specific advertisers for a sales call. One syndication researcher explained this use of the data: "So you ... use that kind of information to get a profile of who is likely to spend in a given type of program or in a given genre—network, syndication, cable—whatever the situation may be" (Interview B: syndication—research). Users of this information recognize its limitations, but they find the reports useful for monitoring the truthfulness of trading partners, competitors, and even their own subordinates within the firm. Sources such as CMR allow buyers and sellers to verify the claims made by others. In effect, the reports act as checks on opportunistic behavior.

The limitations of audience ratings and other types of data do not render the information system ineffective. Market participants trust information when they understand its limitations. For Stinchcombe (1990), a trustworthy system "does not routinely deceive its users about the uncertainty of the conclusions reached on the basis of that information, but does not burden them with information about stable features of the environment" (p. 14). An information system can be trustworthy without providing completely accurate information. Improvements in information quality and quantity are effective to the extent that they decrease uncertainty in a way that is proportional to the time and money spent. But information can never completely eradicate risk.

Personal Interaction

When asked how they keep up with market conditions, several professionals used words similar to those of an ad sales manager: "Just staying in touch with your friends ... really, the easiest way is to pick up the phone. I ran into a customer of mine coming off the train today. The network daytime upfront went down yesterday. I got the whole story from him as I was walking from the car up to Grand Central" (Interview M: syndication—ad sales).

One way for organizations to acquire the information they need to conduct business is through interfirm communication among individuals. Interfirm links are forged at all levels of organization (Granovetter, 1985), and there are many sites for the exchange of information among peers. A few that were mentioned during these interviews are phone conversations, negotiations, cocktail parties, meetings of professional associations, and trade shows. With these opportunities, a small investment of time can yield a significant information advantage. One industry participant offered insight into how these sites are mined when he noted that industry meetings such as NATPE are valuable primarily for "the information moving through the convention" (Interview N: rep firm—programming).

The network of relationships that individuals form in their quest for information is a critical part of the information system that facilitates economic exchange. They are a type of structural response to information problems—a practical and time-efficient way of addressing the friction of which Williamson (1981) wrote. If buyers and sellers share information within networks, then potential problems arising from the costly acquisition of such information are mitigated. Market participants use these networks to gain information such as economic conditions in the marketplace, the location of promising trade opportunities, and the trustworthiness of other market participants (Phalen, 1996, 1998).

In fact, discussions with trading partners and competitors often yield information that is more useful than the sort that comes through more formal channels. The antagonistic interaction (Geertz, 1992), in which each side to an exchange is trying to gain information to create an advantage, actually results in the kind of communication link that keeps information flowing in the marketplace. In this respect, this market resembles the bazaar described by Geertz. Two market participants used very similar words to describe their business. One called it a "street bazaar" (Interview O: national cable network—ad sales); another said, "It's not unlike haggling in the streets in the old days" (Interview P: TV production/distribution—research).

Unwritten rules have developed to facilitate exchange in the market for advertising time. As Kogut, Shan, and Walker (1993) suggested, buyers and sellers learn these rules of cooperation over time, and this knowledge enhances their ability to successfully transact business. A shared understanding between trading partners (see Dore, 1992) works to "make the business tolerable" (Interview N: syndication—ad sales). In fact, market participants indicate that a professional who observes these rules communicates trustworthiness to potential trading partners; and, conversely, one who does not observe them will find it difficult to develop contacts in the marketplace.

The real-world market of television advertising is anything but anonymous. Actors know each other personally, and every transaction is influenced by past interactions and the possibility of future exchange. The likelihood of repeated interaction over time motivates economic actors to "play by the rules" because, as Martin (1993) noted, transactions occur between parties with memories. In other words, there is a path dependence that is intimately linked with the social relationships that emerge from, and exist within, the economy.

Strong relationships and the pattern of repeat business explain why trading partners do not rely on contracts in advertising sales. A sales executive discussed this aspect of the business:

> Everything is done verbally. It is really fairly extraordinary. This business—this part of this business—is fairly extraordinary in that way. That it is really done

on verbal agreements. People spend tens of millions—some even hundreds of millions of dollars based on a conversation and a handshake. And then paperwork may not be generated for months. And it very rarely disintegrates once there is a verbal commitment. It does, but not very often. (Interview Q: syndication—ad sales)

A person's word carries the same weight as a legal document. As another salesperson noted, "Your word is all you have" (Interview R: syndication—ad sales). Even when formal contracts are generated, they seldom require a signature.

The market for television audiences fosters the kind of collaborative-competitive relationships discussed by Powell (1990). Market participants share information with competitors as well as trading partners, and they are aware that their own success is partly dependent on the success of the people with whom they do business. However, the types of relationships formed in different media markets are not identical. Market participants who talked about the relationships between broadcast network salespeople and buyers gave an example. From the perspective of media buyers, driving the hardest bargain doesn't work in the broadcast network arena, but it does work in national spot (see Phalen, 1998).

SUGGESTIONS FOR FURTHER RESEARCH

Information plays an important, if little understood, economic role in electronic media advertising. Buyers and sellers continually exchange two valuable and limited resources—money and time—for the information they need to evaluate potential transactions. However, they know that this information is imperfect. It is asymmetrically available to trading partners, open to misinterpretation, often false or misleading, or too overwhelming for the average decision maker. To deal with this, market participants develop strategies for maximizing the benefits of information relative to the resources of money and time that they invest.

Investing Time and Money to Gain Information. Although many researchers have studied the economics of media markets, there has been little consideration given to the ways that time limitations affect decision making. This analysis suggests several related research questions:

- When do market participants consider an increase in information quality worth the investment of additional resources of money and time?
- What conditions prompt users to demand, and be willing to pay for, higher-quality information from research firms? What types of improvements are generally demanded, and how do they affect the required time investment in data analysis?
- How has the advent of computer technologies affected the time required to gain and analyze information?

- What is the return when market participants invest time and money to attend trade shows or travel to other sites of information exchange? For whom are these sites most useful?

Using Information to Buy Time.   The notion that market participants make trade offs that affect the quality of the information they use suggests several questions for future research:

- What are the differences and similarities between the U.S. information system and the systems of foreign markets? How do these variables affect trade practices in buying and selling advertising time?
- How do variations in audience measurement methodologies among different types of media affect the valuation of commercial time?
- What effect does the institutionalized information system have on the developing "new media" market for advertising time? Will systems uniquely suited to different technologies emerge?
- What are the sources, characteristics, and economic effects of the unwritten rules of business in the market for advertising time?

The answers to these questions will provide a more comprehensive framework for analyzing the economic consequences of trading time and money for information in the television advertising market.

REFERENCES

Coase, R. H. (1937, November). The Nature of the firm. *Economica, 386–405.*

Dore, R. (1992). Goodwill and the spirit of market capitalism. In M. Granovetter & R. Swedberg (Eds.), *The sociology of economic life* (pp. 159–179). Boulder, CO: Westview.

Fournier, G. M., & Martin, D. L. (1983, Spring). Does government-restricted entry produce market power? New evidence from the market for television advertising. *Bell Journal of Economics, 14,* 44–56.

Geertz, C. (1992). The bazaar economy: Information and search in peasant marketing. In M. Granovetter & R. Swedberg (Eds.), *The sociology of economic life* (pp. 225–232). Boulder, CO: Westview.

Granovetter, M. (1985). Economic action and social structure: The problem of embeddedness. *American Journal of Sociology, 91*(3), 481–510.

Jensen, E. (1994, February 4). Networks create ratings test system out of frustration with Nielsen data. *Wall Street Journal,* p. B13.

Kogut, B., Shan, W., & Walker, G. (1993). Knowledge in the network and the network as knowledge: The structuring of new industries. In G. Grabher (Ed.), *The embedded firm: On the socioeconomics of industrial networks* (pp. 67–94). New York: Routledge.

Loveridge, R. (1993, September). Socioeconomics—A bridge too far? *Human Relations, 46,* 1029–1034.

Martin, R. (1993, September). The new behaviorism: A critique of economics and organization. *Human Relations, 46,* 1085–1102.

Phalen, P. F. (1996). *Information and markets and the market for information: An analysis of the market for television audiences.* Unpublished doctoral dissertation, Northwestern University, Evanston, IL.

Phalen, P. F. (1998). The market information system and personalized exchange: Business practices in the market for television audiences. *The Journal of Media Economics, 11*(4), 17–34.

Powell, W. W. (1990). Neither market nor hierarchy: Network forms of organization. *Research in Organizational Behavior, 12,* 295–336.

Stinchcombe, A. L. (1990). *Information and organizations.* Berkeley: University of California Press.

Webster, J. G., & Phalen, P. F. (1994). Victim, consumer or commodity? Audience models in communication policy. In J. Ettema & D. Whitney (Eds.), *Audiencemaking: How the media create the audience* (pp. 19–37). Thousand Oaks, CA: Sage.

Webster, J. G., & Phalen, P. F. (1997). *The mass audience: Rediscovering the dominant model.* Mahwah, NJ: Lawrence Erlbaum Associates.

Williamson, O. E. (1981). The economics of organization: The transaction cost approach. *American Journal of Sociology, 87*(3), 548–577.

Williamson, O. E. (1985). *The economic institutions of capitalism.* New York: the Free Press.

11

TIME AND MEDIA MARKETS:
SUMMARY AND RESEARCH AGENDA[1]

Angel Arrese
University of Navarra

Alan B. Albarran
University of North Texas

In 1999, Peter Kann, publisher of the *Wall Street Journal,* commented in a letter to the Dow Jones shareholders that, of all the information in the Annual Report, what gave him the most pride and satisfaction was the datum referring to the average of 47 minutes that each reader spends on the newspaper. Obviously, this was not significant in itself; instead, its significance had to do with the *Journal's* type of reader, not only affluent and influential, but also probably tremendously busy, with very little time for inconsequential things. Kahn's comment was something more than a rhetorical figure. The Dow Jones business, and of course the *raison d'être* of the *Wall Street Journal,* largely depended on those 47 minutes that around 2 million, mostly subscription-paying readers devoted to the newspaper daily.

That same year, the subscribers' survey at wsj.com, the electronic edition of the newspaper, started with this paragraph: "Busy, online? So are the in-

---

[1]For questions, contact the second author: Dr. Alan B. Albarran, Department of Radio, Television and Film, University of North Texas, P. O. Box 310589, Denton, TX 76203. Phone: 940-565-2537; e-mail: albarran@unt.edu

dividuals who check in with *wsj.com* every morning, throughout the business day and even when they're home at night. Readers of the Wall Street Journal Interactive Edition spend an average of 30 minutes viewing 15 different pages on *wsj.com* every day" (wsj.com Subscriber Study 1999, 2000, p. 3). This time, too, the readers of the electronic edition not only spent their time but also their money navigating the data and information windows of the portal.

Neither the *Wall Street Journal* nor wsj.com are representative examples of the media industry globally; rather, they are special brands in a very peculiar market niche, that of economic and business information. One of the peculiarities of that niche is precisely its sensitivity to the value of readers' time, because these readers are an elite group for whom, almost literally, time is gold. Nevertheless, even for exactly opposite types of information offerings, the time of any kind of person's attention is still one of his or her most valuable assets. Among the most outstanding European journalistic successes in recent years is the free publication *Metro*. It has known how to revive a century-old journalistic formula. The key is precisely its capacity to capture the interest of thousands of people, who are only asked to give some minutes of their otherwise unusable time while traveling from one place to another.

The *Wall Street Journal* and *Metro*, like any other medium or, more generically, like any other media content, compete with an increasingly broad range of information and entertainment that try to capture and hold the daily attention of their target for several minutes of reading. Not only the free and pay media, but also many other activities, vie in that competition for an allocation of each citizen's leisure and work time budgets. Each medium considered globally, each specific support, even each bit of content must demonstrate the attention that it is capable of rousing to justify its existence, to ensure that its demand for attention is satisfied, whether for payment or not. Obviously, the supply of attention is largely limited by human nature, whereas the demand potentially seems to have no limit.

TIME AND MEDIA IN THE ATTENTION ECONOMY

The media market very neatly complies with the principles of the "attention economy," which seem to be spreading to many other sectors. Davenport and Beck commented on this: "Economics, by definition, is the study of how whole societies allocate scarce resources. The scarcest resource for today's business leaders is no longer just land, capital or human labor, and it certainly isn't information. Attention is what's in short supply. And human attention certainly behaves like an economic good in the sense that we buy it and measure it" (Davenport & Beck, 2000, p. 121). Of course, the concept of attention has psychological, biological, and other dimensions that go beyond its simple time consideration, but there can be no doubt that attention and attention time are two sides of the same coin.

Perhaps because comments such as Davenport and Beck's seem so self-evident, time has not been studied enough, as a variable demanding analysis and thought in the media market. At the end of the 1970s, Block echoed this reality: "The allocation of time has not received the attention that it deserves in contemporary mass communication research" (Block, 1979, p. 47). Huysmans addressed the issue much more recently, but from a European prspective, expanding the criticism to aspects beyond the distribution of consumption time: "In 'mainstream' European communication research, no satisfactory conceptual clarification of the relationship between time—as a social construction—and media use has been provided to date" (Huysmans, 1996, p. 483).

The analysis of the media economy is also guilty of forgetting time as a possible explanatory factor of many phenomena related to mass media in general. In the first chapter of this book, Albarran and Arrese revealed that fact, with an analysis of the recent literature on the economics and management of media in the main academic journals. In the large majority of the studies in which time is explicitly a variable, it is a working variable and not the object of the study. In its linear, historical dimension, time is an objective, neuter, exogenous datum needed simply to dynamically analyze processes and changes between different points (in time). This is also the conventional use of time in economics, more as a constant than as a true variable. Physical time—not other possible times, such as psychological or biological time—supposes that there exists one single time, with equal units for everybody and for everything.

This way of seeing time as "clock time" also makes it possible to consider time as a special unit of measurement, which constitutes the second fundamental sphere of studies that emphasize the time variable in the analysis of information markets. Time-budget studies and time-use studies are different generic research approaches that focus on the use of time as a unit of measurement to analyze social, organizational, economic, and other types of realities (see Ver Ploeg et al., 2000). In these cases, time is treated as a scarce and therefore valuable commodity, susceptible to multiple uses. With great common sense, Von Mises highlighted this economic dimension of time: "Man is subject to the passing of time. He comes into existence, grows, becomes old, and passes away. His time is scarce" (as cited in McKenzie, 1997). Becker (1965) developed a first theoretical approximation to the allocation of time among different activities from an economic perspective, which was followed by other attempts at a deeper understanding of the economy of time (DeSerpa, 1971; O'Driscoll & Rizzo, 1996; Sharp, 1981).

Mass media, of course, are just one more of the many activities that demand and consume people's meager time. Like any other human activity, they can be studied from this perspective (Hornick & Schlinger, 1981). The great peculiarity in the consumption of media in respect of many other consumer activities is the singular value that the accumulation of consumption times has traditionally had in this market. In addition to the income generated by the direct sale of products and services, the media economy has largely depended on its capacity to sell to third parties the attention time that it can capture. It is significant that precisely the media are used as a paradigm of organization guided by the principles of the attention economy, or of the so-called "attention industries" (Davenport & Beck, 2000). Conversely, as Vogel (1998) commented, the cost of time and the consumption-time intensity of entertainment (media) goods and services are very significant factors when selecting among alternatives. It is significant that Vogel began his book *Entertainment Industry Economics* precisely by quoting from the Bible the book of *Ecclesiastes*: "To everything there is a season, and a time to every purpose under the heaven."

Both the study of time in processes and changes, and the use of time as a unit of measurement in media consumption, are fundamental aspects for media studies, especially in this age of information overload. Although they are the most common, they are not the only relevant issues posed by the consideration of time in the information markets.

The mass media play an essential role in the processes of social construction of reality, and the very temporal configuration of media and messages have transcendental effects on the lives of millions of people. Huysmans (1996), with an eye to developing a social science conceptualization of time for communication research on media use, highlighted three fundamental directions for research in this field: a macro approach theorizing the impact of media on sociocultural evolution and human time consciousness, a micro/macro approach dealing with temporal qualities of mediated messages and the temporal organization of the message production process, and a micro approach dealing with the media use in the temporal context of everyday life. The second research approach especially considers temporal aspects of the media themselves with clear implications for the media economy, particularly with respect to the management of companies and mass media. In fact, the temporal qualities of the various contents and their effects on the management of companies and mass media have been, if this is possible, an even more neglected subject than that of the time dimensions of the consumption of media. This is another aspect in which the communication sector has behaved the same as other sectors. In a study on organizational theory, Goddard commented, "Organizational theorists have failed to examine how time is perceived and used in organizations" (Goddard, 2001, p. 19).

The contributors of this volume, from various perspectives and research traditions, tried to approach some of the interesting aspects posed by the consideration of time as the backbone of analysis in the study of the media market and economy. Although their levels of analysis differed, they all emphasized the relevance of the time dimensions for a better comprehension of the media market. In some cases, they proposed innovative ways to analyze time. At the same time, some studies pointed out clear limitations for considering the media from the perspective of time, limitations that have to do with theoretical (time conceptualization) as well as practical aspects (time measurement and management).

THE ELUSIVE NATURE AND THE IMPLICATIONS OF TIME IN MEDIA MARKETS

Jacques Durand's chapter (chap. 2, "Media and Representations of Time") served, to some extent, to contextualize the broad range of subjects and the depth of the implications of considering the time dimensions of the media. Based on the traditional research on time budgets, Durand pondered the effects of the time of exposure to the media, not so much from an economic perspective but instead from a sociological point of view. The various perceptions of time manifested in the media, and their task of restructuring the time of current events and of life through fiction, affect their attitude toward the consumers' time. One of the conclusions of the study was that the media manage to treat as relative two essential characteristics of time: irreversibility and divergence. Although it is important to take into account the linear conception of a time that is the same for everybody, the media somehow constitute a fundamental element in the process of establishing time as relative. Albert Einstein once referred to this psychological attribute of time by saying that when a man sits with a woman for an hour it seems like a minute. But let him sit on a hot stove for a minute, and it's longer than an hour. That's relativity.

Those various ways of experiencing time have implications for comprehending essential aspects of the media economy. This book addressed at least three fields of study in which the analysis of temporal aspects can shed new light on this matter. In the first place, several chapters concentrated on the management of time as an essential aspect of media management (Picard & Grönlund, chap. 4; Shaver & Shaver, chap. 5; Medina, chap. 6); second, two studies developed, from various perspectives, aspects of competition in the media market such as competing for audience time (Mac-Donald & Dimmick, chap. 3; Nieto, chap. 9); finally, another group of chapters concentrated their analyses on the economic value of time as a particularly relevant measure of value in the media market (Goff, chap. 7; Pérez-Latre, chap. 8; Phalen, chap. 10).

Time Management and Media Management

Given the diverse temporal nature that defines their content, the management of the different mass media has peculiarities worth taking into account. Picard and Grönlund pointed this out in chapter 4 when they referred to the variety of sensitivities that the various media have to time in their production and content distribution activities. For a couple of decades, CNN has provided a good example of how a medium such as television can transform its sensitivity to time. The novel way of managing time by scheduling news 24 hours a day, practically all over the planet, allowed that network to create a new mode for television, as Mercedes Medina explained in chapter 6.

The improvement of time management in all the processes of developing and distributing content is also one of the advantages that justify phenomena such as today's growing convergence and corporate concentration in the media industries. In chapter 5, Mary Alice Shaver and Dan Shaver showed the impact that corporate concentration and multimedia convergence—intimately related phenomena—have on achieving managerial efficiencies of time and cost.

From the point of view of information company management, the last three studies emphasized the importance of overcoming the barriers of time and space that traditionally have differentiated some media from others, and that still constitute limitations with important managerial implications. The concentration of media companies, the convergence of content, the progress of the telecommunications networks (with the Internet at the head), and processes such as the globalization of the markets all tend to lead to overcoming those barriers. Thus, it is understandable that some European countries, such as Great Britain and Germany, have begun to look at a matter of undoubted concern—the concentration of information companies—not only from economic perspectives, but also by considering the percentage of media consumption time (independent of the type of medium) that some multimedia groups can accumulate compared to the total consumption of the population (Iosifides, 1997).

Time Competition and Media Competition

The analysis of *media time budgets* poses new ways of studying the competition and the substitution relationships among various media in the markets. Just as it is possible to make an economic analysis that takes into account the weight of the various content industries in each market and the competitive relationships among them, it is also feasible to consider the various content offerings of each medium from the perspective of their capacity to competitively capture people's time.

In chapter 9, Alfonso Nieto suggested considering media markets as time markets, in which the various contents compete for the scarce time that people relinquish subject to certain limitations, depending on their socioeconomic characteristics. This chapter focused on analyzing the time supply for the traditional media in the Spanish market, emphasizing some significant differences among regions. Professor Nieto performed an aggregate analysis that considered average consumption times for press, radio, and television. This study pointed to the need to qualify the times devoted to the different media depending on socioeconomic and geographical variables, as well as the composition of the time portfolio allocated to the various media by the audience.

In a more micro approach, based on the theory of the niche (which suggests that media compete for limited resources), in chapter 3 MacDonald and Dimmick undertook the analysis of the time shift between the consumption of Internet and that of television. Their chapter not only addressed one of the most timely issues from the point of view of the competition among media (the effect of the Internet on the consumption of traditional media), but also demonstrated how important time analysis is to this type of market. Partially replacing consumption of certain media for others can, in many cases, materialize in the reorganization of the monetary resources that people allocate to each content supplier. However, in all cases, that replacement entails a redistribution of the consumption time. When the importance of the monetary redistribution is minimal, as in the consumption of certain media (e.g., the Internet and television), the analysis of the time redistribution is essential.

Both Nieto's and MacDonald and Dimmick's studies called our attention to some of the problems that arise when considering media markets as time markets. One of those problems, perhaps one of the most important, is the measurement of consumption time. Whether mechanical procedures are used or measurements are based on recall, the knowledge of the quantity and the quality of time actually devoted to the various media will certainly be disparate. This is also one of the core limitations for the economic appraisal of media consumption time.

Time Value and Money Value

The electronic media have a long tradition in the use of time consumption as a unit of economic value because, after all, the concept of audience is no more than a certain accumulation of qualified times. Based on that accumulation of times, broadcast time is bought and sold for the advertising content. Nevertheless, as Patricia Phalen explained in chapter 10, in spite of this being one of the markets with the most developed time appraisal techniques, a great many deficiencies must be rectified, or at least their impact must be minimized. The time consumption measurement and appraisal systems for television content, which support a good part of the advertising market, are inflicted with quite substantial shortcomings; the technical solution for these is far from simple.

In fact, the advertising market and the decisions of the media planning professionals, often based on qualitative estimates, demonstrate time and again how the economic value of television time consumption eludes the simple objective measurement of accumulated exposure times. There are almost infinite possibilities for setting the price of one same unit of time on different scheduling grids, on different channels, for different advertisers, during different periods.

The capacity of the new technologies to facilitate the distinction between passive time and active time is undermining the very concept of media planning and the assessment that has been made of media time consumption up until now. In chapter 8, Pérez-Latre pondered the importance of interactivity as a new variable in the appraisal of media consumption and its possible effects on the distribution of advertising content in the future. Undoubtedly, the interactive potential of the Internet and digital technologies has had a major role in triggering this new concern about the nature of media consumption time.

Along this same line of thinking about the new challenges that the Internet and new technologies pose for the economic assessment of media time consumption, chapter 7 expounded on some European experiences of charging consumers directly for the time they spend consuming media content. In this chapter, David Goff developed some of the elements of the debate between the income models of Internet providers based on flat rates (which allow network access for unlimited time) and the models that charge per time of use (inherited from the business model of the telecommunications industry). This debate is still open. It focuses the problem of the economic assessment of time consumption of content beyond the consideration of the cost of access and use of the infrastructure.

Taken together, the variety of topics dealt with in the chapters of this book reflects how the mass media and information companies need to delve deeply into their nature as suppliers of content with a growing leading role in the attention economies. Many are already doing so, but others have a long way to go. Returning to the anecdote related at the beginning of this chapter, the paltry interest that the print media world has traditionally taken, at least from academic perspectives, in the analysis of the quantity and the quality of reading time is remarkable. Reading time is starting to displace circulation figures as the key variable for assessing competitive offerings in attention markets. In Spain, for example, only in recent years has this begun to be considered a relevant datum in the various surveys on media use that the market employs. Recently in the United States, the Readership Institute, under the direction of John Lavine, has carried out a national study on the reading of the press in which the concept of readership is revised and redefined as time spent, frequency, and completeness (Readership Institute, 2001).

Considering the media globally, studies such as the *Average Consumption in America* (Mediaweek and Fairfield Research), or the *Communications Industry Forecast* (Veronis, Suhler & Associates, 2000), pay special attention to time as a variable in their analyses of the content industries. One of the forecasts in Veronis, Shuler and Associates' 2000 report explained:

> Fueled by increases in time spent on Internet, video games and recorded music, the average number of hours spent per person on media supported predominantly by consumers increased 31.3 percent from 1995 to 1999, reaching 1,329 hours in 1999. Time spent per person on media with significant advertiser support dropped 8.5 percent in the same period to 2,069 hours last year. We project that hours spent per person on media supported predominantly by consumers will grow 29.1 percent to 1,716 hours from 1999 to 2004, while time spent with media with significant advertiser support will remain relatively stagnant, inching up less than 1 percent to 2,070 hours per person. (Veronis, Shuler & Associates, 2000, p. 37)

Approaches like those described, all with patent professional orientation and focusing on the analysis of media consumption time, must be complemented with research and academic reflection on the many time dimensions that operate in the media markets.

DIRECTIONS FOR FURTHER RESEARCH

This book identified three spheres for research that use time as a key study variable to shed new light on some of the traditional topics dealt with by media economy. Time management and media management, time competition and media competition, and time value and money value constitute generic areas of study that allow various theoretical and practical analyses. Nevertheless, beyond the specific topics that can be studied in each area, the basic issues revolving around the conceptualization and methodological ways to operationalize time in the media need to be researched more deeply.

From a theoretical point of view, more research into the peculiarities of use and consumption time of each medium and its relationship with contextual elements—venue, situation, relationship with other activities, and so on—is called for. It is necessary to qualify the time devoted to the various media before proceeding to any comparative analysis or study of time consumption replacement between different types of content and media. In this regard, the study of time media budgets should be enriched with the findings arising out of the growing attention to researching time budgets in general. In addition to the objective dimensions of time as clock time, we need a deeper understanding of the cultural and psychological dimensions of media consumption time, because they largely determine the perception that the various audiences have of that consumption. It must not be forgotten that in addition to the mechanical registering of electronic media consumption time (with all the technical problems that those systems entail), a good part of the research on media consumption is based on recall. Media consumption surveys generally reflect perceptions that are more or less close to reality, but, in any case, are determined by the special experience that the consumption of each medium provides.

Finally, another time aspect normally left out of analyses of media consumption is that of the repetition of the consumption over time. Loyalty, as a display of confidence manifested in the reiteration of certain people's consumption times toward certain media and content, acquires a special value in attention economies.

To gain a deeper understanding of those time dimensions of media consumption and convert them to operational variables for decision making, more empirical research is required to identify time as a fundamental backbone of any analysis. Both the professional as well as the academic fields have quite heterogeneous information on consumption times of the various media. In some cases, as happens with the print media, reading has been vaguely defined as a simple frequency of reading (read yesterday, during the last week, in the last month). The same has occurred with media such as the radio. In contrast, the electronic media have had at least a double measurement (audience meter registers plus surveys), although, in this field too, opportunities to improve the measurement systems are evident.

But although we have a generally good understanding of time allocation as applied to the media regarding ratings and circulation data, there is much to be learned given a greater emphasis on the temporal dimension. First, let us consider the individual level of analysis. Contemporary media research is particularly lacking in longitudinal studies or panel designs, even though early communication research featured several seminal studies (e.g., Katz & Lazarsfeld, 1955; Lazarsfeld, Berelson, & Gaudet, 1968). Longitudinal designs would enable researchers to gain a greater understanding and awareness of changing patterns, preferences, and tastes over time, especially regarding allocation of time.

Cohort analysis represents an alternative to longitudinal panel designs but, again, the research using this methodology is scarce. In cohort analysis, researchers study how variables change among different age groups or cohorts over time. It is not necessary for the same people to be studied at different time intervals, as in longitudinal or panel designs, because the focus is on particular cohorts. An excellent example of cohort analysis is Dimmick, McCain, and Bolton's study (1979) of changes in media use over the life span, using different age cohorts.

Finally, the growing expansion of media-related technologies—from the use of the Internet to devices like personal digital assistants—all impact the time, attention, and advertising dollars devoted to media markets. However, to date our research is descriptive and does not detail the processes involved in how someone decides to use his or her time, nor the differences that may occur across age groups, genders, or ethnic lines. Expectations call for further fragmentation of the audience, but research remains primarily descriptive.

At the group/industry level, research has relied primarily on trend-based studies to assess the impact of certain variables over time. Borrowing from Kline (1977), most of the research has considered time as a setting and not as a sequence of events. In other words, the emphasis has been on description rather than analysis and inference. There are numerous areas in which this approach could yield richer and more enlightening data. For example, policy studies could gain from this line of inquiry. By looking at underlying causes and inferences, researchers gain a different perspective of exactly how regulatory decisions evolve.

Economic studies could also benefit from such an approach. These studies would provide far richer analysis if researchers would consider sequences as opposed to just the setting of events. Studies related to management and changes in corporate culture are other areas ripe for this type of research.

Finally, we consider the global level of analysis. The globalization of the media industries lends itself to many potential studies that might consider time as a variable of study. Trend-based research and time-series analysis, as well as how globalization impacts the political and economic processes over time, are natural areas of study. Furthermore, the ways that different cultures approach work and leisure time have a direct bearing on the success of media companies as they move away from their domestic borders. Analyzing globalization from a temporal dimension can only add to our understanding of this important phenomenon.

REFERENCES

Becker, G. S. (1965). A theory of the allocation of time. *Economic Journal, 75,* 493–517.

Block, M. P. (1979). Time allocation in mass communication research. In M. J. Voigt & G. J. Hannemann (Eds.), *Progress in communication sciences* (Vol. 1, pp. 29–50). Norwood, NJ: Ablex.

Davenport, T. H., & Beck, J. C. (2000, September-October). Getting the attention you need. *Harvard Business Review,* pp. 119–126.

DeSerpa, A. C. (1971). A theory of the economics of time. *Economic Journal, 81,* 828–846.

Dimmick, J., McCain, T., & Bolton, T. (1979). Media use and the life span. *American Behavioral Scientist, 23*(1), 7–32.

Goddard, R. (2001). Time in organizations. *Journal of Management Development, 20*(1), 19–27.

Hornick, J., & Schlinger, M. J. (1981). Allocation of time to the mass media. *Journal of Consumer Research, 7,* 343–355.

Huysmans, F. (1996). Social time and media use. *Communications, 21*(4), 483–505.

Iosifides, P. (1997). Methods of measuring media concentration. *Media, Culture & Society, 19*(4), 643–664.

Katz, E., & Lazarsfeld, P. (1955). *Personal influence. The part played by people in the flow of mass communications.* Glencoe, IL: Free Press.

Kline, F. G. (1977). Time in communication research. In P. M. Hirsch, P. V. Miller, & F. G. Kline (Eds.), *Strategies for communications research* (pp. 187–204). Beverly Hills, CA: Sage.

Lazarsfeld, P., Berelson, B., & Gaudet, H. (1968). *The people's choice. How the voter makes up his mind in a presidential campaign.* New York: Columbia University Press.

McKenzie, R. B. (1997). *The nature of time in economics.* Retrieved September 23, 2000 from http://www.gsm.uci.edu/~mckenzie/nature.htm

O'Driscoll, G. P., & Rizzo, M. J. (1996). *The economics of time and ignorance.* London: Routledge.

Readership Institute. (2001). *Impact Study.* Retrieved September 10, 2001 from http://readership.org

Sharp, C. H. (1981). *The economics of time.* Oxford: Martin Robertson.

Ver Ploeg, M., Altoni, J., Bradburn, N., Devanzo, J., Nordhaus, W., & Samaniego, F. (2000). *Time-use measurement and research.* Washington: Committee on National Statistics, National Research Council.

Veronis, Shuler & Associates. (2000). *Communications industry forecast.* New York: Author.

Vogel, H. L. (1998). *Entertainment industry economics. A guide for financial analysis* (4th ed.). Cambridge, UK: Cambridge University Press.

wsj.com Subscriber Study. (1999). Retrieved October 20, 2000 from http://info.wsj.com

AUTHOR INDEX

A

Albarran, A. B.,31, *46*
Altoni, J., 163, *171*
Aristotle, 5, *11*
Attali, J., 16, *26*

B

Baker, S., 103, *108*
Bale, T., 91, *94*
Baran, S., 83, 84, 85, *94*
Barthes, R., *26*
Bates, B. J., 66, *78*
Bazin, A., 23, *26*
Beck, J. C., 162, 164, *171*
Becker, G. S., 7, *11*, 163, *171*
Becker, L., 49, *60*
Beesley, M. E., 81, *92*
Belleret, R., 18, *26*
Belson, W. A., 7, *11*
Berelson, B., 170, *171*
Berendt, A., 98, *108*
Berger, C. Q., 29, *47*
Berger, G., 24, *27*
Berne, E., 17, *27*
Block, M. P., 7, *11*, 31, *46*, 163, *171*
Blumenthal, H., 88, *93*
Bogart, L., 30, *46*, 123, *125*
Bolton, T., 170, *171*
Borzo, J., 97, 98, 101, 106, *108*
Bourdieu, P., 24, *27*
Boyd-Barret, O., 87, *93*
Bradburn, N., 163, *171*
Brodesser, C., 67, *78*
Brody, J. H., 51, *60*

Brown, R., 90, *93*
Brown, S., 65, *78*
Brown, W., 39, *46*
Busterna, J., 64, *78*

C

Cache, B., 14, *27*
Cairncross, F., 92, *93*
Cavallaro, M., 103, *108*
Chaguiboff, J., 21, *27*
Chan, K., 106, *108*
Chan-Olmsted, S., 66, *78*
Chapelain, B., 21, *27*
Charpin, F., 14, *27*
Chyi, H. I., 70, *78*
Coase, R. H., 145, *158*
Cohen, A. A., 88, 91, *93*
Colombo, F., 84, 91, *93*
Conde, F., 137, 138, *144*
Costa de Beauregard, O., 19, *27*
Cousido, P., 129, *144*
Cunningham, 30, 34, *46*

D

Daniel, C., 103, *108*
Davenport, T. H., 162, 164, *171*
Davies, P., 5, 6, *11*
Debray, R., 17, *27*
DeSerpa, A. C., 7, *11*, 163, *171*
Devanzo, J., 163, *171*
Dewerth-Pallmeyer, D., 49, *60*
Dimmick, J., 31, 33, *46*, 170, *171*
Donnat, O., 15, 18, *27*
Dore, R., 156, *158*

173

Subject Index